MANSIONS of DENVER

MANSIONS *of* DENVER

The Vintage Years 1870–1938

JAMES BRETZ

PRUETT PUBLISHING COMPANY
BOULDER, COLORADO

Printed in the United States of America

11 10 09 08 07 06 05   5 4 3 2 1

Library of Congress Cataloging-in-Publication Data

Bretz, James, 1948-
 The mansions of Denver : the vintage years / James Bretz.-- 1st ed.
     p. cm.
 Includes bibliographical references.
 ISBN 0-87108-937-8 (alk. paper)
 1. Mansions--Colorado--Denver--History--19th century. 2. Mansions--Colorado--Denver--History--20th century. 3. Denver (Colo.)--Buildings, structures, etc. I. Title.

NA7511.4.D46B74 2004
728.8'09788'83--dc22

                    2004015200

Design & Composition by MacWorks Inc

To:

JAMES E. NICHOLS
MY UNCLE

THE WORLD WILL NOT SOON FORGET WHAT HAPPENED TO ROME.

TABLE OF CONTENTS

ACKNOWLEDGMENTS

I would like to express my appreciation to the expert staff of the Denver Public Library Western History Department for their help in the researching of this book. Among those who shared their knowledge and expertise were Bruce Hanson, John Irwin, James Jeffrey, Jim Kroll, Phil Panum, Janice Prater, Brent Wagner, Barbara Walton, and Kay Wisnia. Special thanks to Colleen Nunn, who often went out of her way to steer me in the right direction. Jim and Diane Peiker and Melissa Feher-Peiker provided much of the background for the Raymond House/Castle Marne.

Rebecca Lintz, Barbara Dey, Debra Neiswomger, and Karyl Klein, all staff of the Colorado Historical Society, generously shared their wealth of information pertaining to the buildings and history of early Denver and provided many of the vintage photographs that appear in this book. Rick Bass read, and re-read, the first drafts and gave his usual sensible advice. Sharon McIntyre planted the seed for this book and gave me her honest criticisms as it developed. Margot Crowe supplied much of the history of the Bohm House/Holiday Chalet. John C. Mulvihill provided photographic material and historical background on the Campion family and made corrections to my original manuscript.

Thanks go to Dick Kreck of the *Denver Post* for sharing his knowledge of Isabel Patterson Springer and the Brown Palace murders. Arlene Hirschfeld was kind enough to provide information relating to Shangri-La. Newell Grant was helpful with the James B. Grant/A.E. Humphreys and Edwin B. Hendrie chapters and made corrections to my original material. Thanks to Dorothy Bowie, attorney Wade Eldridge, and Dan Thorsnes. Irene Gay shared her recollections of the Edwin B. Hendrie house and provided family background. Mr. and Mrs. Gerald Priddy supplied background information pertaining to the Richtofen castle. Thanks also to Walt Keller of the Lumber Baron Inn, attorney Michael Sawaya, Mark and Diane Hayden, Mary Ebrahimi, Herb Hoard, and Dr. Thomas Williams, Curator of Phipps Conference Center, University of Denver.

INTRODUCTION

"**M**iles of Fine Homes" was the headline of a January 1893 issue of the *Denver Republican* newspaper. Denver was proud of its growing wealth and prestige, and numerous newspaper articles of the day touted the newest and finest houses built in the city, along with drawings and photos and endless descriptions of the interior appointments. This made for entertaining reading for the city's middle class, who treated the city's wealthy as the Europeans did royalty. The article continued:

> Denver is a city of homes—a beautiful city of beautiful homes. It is this fact which among other facts most quickly strikes the visitor. Richard Harding Davis wrote a chapter about Denver in his book of Western travels, and among other things he said: "The two most striking things about the city to me were the public schools and the private houses. Great corporations, insurance companies and capitalists erect twelve story buildings everywhere—In Denver there are not only the big buildings, but mile after mile of separate houses, and of the prettiest, strictest and most proper architecture." This is Denver's fame and every year adds to it. It would be an impossible task to attempt any enumeration of the hundreds of beautiful residences. The most that can be done is to pick from the long lists some of the conspicuous ones to serve as example of the best.

In an age when vast fortunes were made almost overnight, mostly from the gold and silver being dug out of the hills above Denver, and from the burgeoning industries that helped to support the booming population, the show of great wealth was treated almost as a sport. The city's upper class displayed little restraint as they bought up fine carriages, fancy clothes, and, of course, the most lavish living accommodations money could buy. As one mansion went up, another one followed, only it was bigger and more expensive. Another came after that, until it seemed there would be no end to it. The captains of industry originally chose downtown Denver as its environ, and, as commerce pushed them out, Capitol Hill became the neighborhood of choice.

Astonishingly, of the hundreds of mansions erected between 1880 and 1920 in the downtown area and in Capitol Hill, relatively few survive.

Some of these monuments to money remained with their original owners for only a few years before being converted to commercial use or being destroyed. Fortunes were lost, people died, or owners moved to the country or out of state. Heirs tired of the burden of maintaining huge mansions and gave them up, moving to more manageable quarters. The impact of commerce had a great effect on the dynamics of city living where the monied families were concerned. Other factors, such as high taxes, staffing problems, and the general trend, especially after World War II, to economize and downsize, were all deciding factors in the disappearance of these structures.

As these residences were vacated, there were but few options for their continued use. Many became schools, dormitories, or institutions, which was the case for most of the earliest residences in the downtown area, while the rest were converted for use as boardinghouses, or "guest hotels." By the 1950s, while many of these structures were still left standing, they had served utilitarian purposes for so long that it was almost impossible to ever think of them as being single-family homes. Even today, one tends to think of the city's surviving mansions in terms of business offices or apartments.

Starting in the late 1950s and escalating in the 1960s, and also as part of Denver's urban-renewal project, demolition of many of Denver's finest homes was carried out in earnest. In an era when such destruction was ignored by the general populace, developers and investors were more or less indiscriminate in their haste to clear land for future development. Mansions and lesser houses fell at an astonishing rate, like rows of dominoes. Historical significance played little part in any preservation efforts, nor did architectural integrity or size or quality of craftsmanship. These hulking reminders of an era long gone were in the way of progress, and progress meant money. These houses stood like so many white elephants, too big to maintain as private residences, too costly to update, and too old to use for a majority of purposes. Astonishingly, many were bulldozed into the ground, and their hand-carved mantels, stained-glass windows, ornamental plasterwork, and marble flooring all became one with the landfill. Few elements were saved except for copper and brass piping and other metalwork that was deemed salvageable by the demolition crews.

In 1963, in response to the announcement that the former John Campion mansion, at 800 Logan Street, and one-time headquarters of the Denver chapter of the Red Cross, was to be torn down, Eleanore Weckbaugh, one of the city's more vocal socialites, wrote to the *Denver Post* with the following lambast: "Has the city that I love gone completely insane? I worked at the Campion house for four years in the Red Cross Motor Corps. What is happening to this state and the city fathers that they cannot do something to stop this organized vandalism? We shall have nothing but apartment houses with blue waste baskets hanging out the windows. They all look alike, from Golden to east Denver."

She was not the only one asking that question. Many of the preservation groups with which we are now familiar, such as Historic Denver, Inc., did not exist at the time or were in their infancy. To be sure, many of the mansions were demolished early on, beginning in the 1910s and 1920s, as land use varied and property values escalated. Such was the case of the property surrounding the State Capitol Building. Once ringed by fine Victorian residences—including those belonging to Mrs. Horace Tabor at Seventeenth and Broadway, Albert Welch at Grant Street and Colfax Avenue, Governor Job Cooper at 1500 Grant Street, and the home of William N. Byers, editor of the *Rocky Mountain News*, at the northeast corner of Colfax Avenue and Sherman Street—commerce dictated a change in land use, and owners moved out. The Tabor site was used for construction of storefronts; the Welch house was demolished to make way for the Argonaut Hotel; the Cooper house was demolished for a filling station, and later, a bank building; and the Byers property became the site of a state municipal building in about 1920. Mansions to the north of this area survived for a time, but in only a few decades most had been wrecked.

Early attempts at preservation were often futile at best. A case in point was the huge Harold Bellamy house at 1175 Race Street, on the east edge of Cheesman Park. This home was razed in the mid-1970s for a luxury high-rise. The house was typical of those being destroyed to make way for high-rise apartment buildings that were slowly making their way around the perimeter of the park, ever since the area was zoned R-3 in the 1950s. Cheesman Park had been ringed with large mansions on the east, west, and north sides, with large homes lining both sides of Franklin Street Parkway to the south. The home owners along Humboldt Street, on the west edge, banded together and lobbied to have their neighborhood designated as a historic district. This was later done, effectively protecting the integrity and future of the neighborhood. Homes along the east and north edges suffered a fate far different. The Bellamy house, built around 1900, represented to many the glaring need to establish some limits on development and to raise public awareness of the need to preserve the city's heritage. As the house was faced with demolition, many of the neighbors banded together at the behest of Bill Pace, a neighborhood activist who lived nearby. The group protested the increase in high-rises circling the park and the destruction of the historic houses wrecked to make way for these luxury apartments and condos. The Chester S. Morey mansion, long a Denver landmark, was wrecked just up the street at 1075 Race Street. Morey had been president of the Morey Mercantile Company and had previously lived in a mansion at 1555 Sherman Street that was demolished to make way for the Farmer's Union Building in the mid-1950s. Many of the mansions on the north side of the park had been similarly razed. This was the dawning of awareness that Denver was losing something special, something irreplaceable. But it was a dilemma not easily solved.

The Space Age, especially, was a time of looking forward with anticipation and excitement, not a time to look to the past. This was especially apparent from the extremely low prices at which many of these houses sold, often for just a fraction of their original cost and sometimes just for the value of the land itself.

By the 1970s, preservation found an unlikely ally in Mary Rae. Rae had been in the real-estate business, specializing in the restoration and conversion of older properties for commercial use, something that had, for the most part, been previously ignored. In 1978, she had a large house moved from 1127 Race Street, an area that was rapidly being developed with high-rise condos, to a lot in the 1300 block of High Street. In another impressive move later that same year, she had a large house moved from 818 Pearl Street to the southwest corner of Tenth Avenue and Emerson Street, to complement and complete a condo project there. For a time she ran her business out of a mansion at 950 Logan Street.

Mansion Properties, Inc., another real-estate company with a mind toward preservation, was formed with the intention of buying up vintage properties and either restoring them or converting them for commercial use. One of its first successes was the conversion of the Tears-McFarlane house at 1200 Williams Street, redone for office use. Two of the company's other early conversions were the Oscar Malo mansion at Eighth Avenue and Pennsylvania Street, and the John Porter mansion at Eighth Avenue and Pearl Street.

The most drastic attempt at preservation in recent memory was the removal of the John Milheim mansion from its roost at 1355 Pennsylvania Street to its present site at 1515 Race Street. The 5,000-square-foot, five-bedroom house, slated for demolition in the late 1980s, was saved at the eleventh hour by two enterprising young men, Ralph Heronema, a real-estate broker, and his partner, Jim Alleman. After the house had served its run as a boardinghouse and apartments, the Colorado State Employees Credit Union bought it and wanted to expand on the property. The process of moving the 500-ton structure from its foundation, north on Pennsylvania Street and east on Colfax Avenue to Race Street, was a feat in itself, and the site attracted throngs of bystanders. Colfax took on the look and feel of a parade, and even though the entire process was slow and painstaking, and took more than a week, many onlookers returned every day to watch the progress. Traffic was diverted and power lines were temporarily moved to make way for the massive structure. The move cost $400,000, but the owners felt justified. Heronema told the press that Denver was losing vintage houses at an alarming rate; one had to be saved occasionally.

By the 1990s, the idea had caught on that there was, indeed, a way to preserve some of Denver's early architectural gems and focus on the future at the same time. It is, today, quite common to find old residences and other buildings that have been converted to modern use as medical offices, law offices, lofts and condos, and, ironically, private residences.

The John Milheim house slowly makes its way down the middle of Colfax Avenue.

Author's Collection

FROM DOWNTOWN TO CAPITOL HILL

F or many of those who made their fortunes in the region in the last quarter of the nineteenth century, Denver was the most likely place to settle. It was a growing and vital city and held the promise of a great future. Most of these wealthy men chose to build their homes in what is now the downtown Denver area, in the days when it was a heavy mix of commercial and residential structures. In the 1870s and 1880s, many fine homes sprang up next to livery stables, wagon-making shops, blacksmithing shops, theaters, hotels, and even saloons. The elite of the day chose Fourteenth Street as their exclusive avenue, even though it was nothing more than a quiet dirt road; it was far enough removed from the noise and bustle of the rest of downtown to be considered a fashionable area. Along this street lived Nathaniel Hill, mining investor, smelter owner, and U.S. senator; David H. Moffat, railroad tycoon; and John Evans, second territorial governor of the state and patriarch of one of Denver's most prominent families. His children and grandchildren became involved in many important aspects of the city, from utilities and transportation to the support of the Denver Art Museum and the restoration of the Central City Opera House. Walter S. Cheesman, owner of the monopolistic Denver Union Water Company, lived downtown. So did real-estate tycoon Henry C. Brown, builder of the Brown Palace Hotel and owner of a large tract that included the future site of the State Capitol. Thomas Patterson, owner and editor of the *Rocky Mountain News*, built a Victorian pile at Seventeenth and Welton streets, while early Denver mayor Wolfe Londoner lived

The home of David Moffat on Fourteenth Street in downtown Denver.

farther north on Champa Street. The home of early pioneer William Barth was located at the northeast corner of Sixteenth and Stout streets. It was built in 1869 and torn down in 1887 to make way for the Barth Building. Adjacent was the fine home of Dr. Frederick Bancroft. It was purchased as a gift by his wife's father and was later demolished to make way for the A.T. Lewis Department Store. Dr. Bancroft was the grandfather of Caroline Bancroft, popular Denver historian and author.

The William B. Daniels house, built in 1880 at 1422 Curtis Street, was eccentric even in its own day. It was described by a reporter of the era as an adaptation of many architectural styles, with a roof of slate and windows of galvanized iron. The basement contained fuel rooms, a kitchen, and a dining room. The main floor consisted of a "gentlemen's hall," double parlors, and a lavatory. The second floor held four bedrooms and baths, "all being finished in late styles of work, fitted with grates and wood mantles complete."

William Bradley Daniels made his way west from New York in the 1860s and settled in Denver, establishing a dry-goods store with J.M. Echart. The business flourished at Fifteenth and Blake streets. The store carried a wide variety of merchandise such

The home of John Sidney Brown in downtown Denver.

The odd design of the William B. Daniels house made it stand out even in its day.

as clothing, shoes, furniture and carpeting. Echart died in the 1870s, and Daniels found a new partner in William Fisher. The men soon purchased two lots at Sixteenth and Lawrence streets and, in 1878, built a four-story building that became the hub of Denver shopping. Daniels and Fisher were the merchant princes of the West.

After Daniels' death in 1890, the house was purchased by Ed Chase, Denver's gambling kingpin, and turned into the Inter-Ocean Club, one of Chase's many gambling houses in the area. A long arrest record followed Chase to Denver, but by this time he had learned to skate around the police. He

was able to attend to his various illicit concerns with little interference, for the most part, and even gained a modicum of respectability. The house was completely redone to suit the needs of the business, including luxurious carpets, tapestries, and red velvet drapes. Slot machines were installed along with tables for poker and dice games. The rooms were arranged so that, in the event of a police visit, most of the incriminating evidence could be concealed in a hurry. Chase also occasionally posted one of his men in the glass-enclosed cupola, which made an ideal lookout tower. A newspaper article at the time declared: "Brain Will Be Bewildered by Array of Costly Fittings While the Tin Horns and Licensed

The James Archer house was later used as the Denver Municipal Dispensary, and for a time it was used by the Colorado University Medical School.

Looters Deliberately Rob the Tipsy Victim." And many men lost all their money, and more, until the house was finally shut down. It was converted to a rooming house in 1907 and was razed in the mid-1920s to make way for the new, multistory Mountain States Telephone Company building. That building, considered an architectural marvel when it opened in 1929, is still in use by the company today.

In 1939, two old houses were wrecked that stood opposite the Mountain States Telephone Company building. One was built by Major John Fillmore, who was an army paymaster dispatched to the West to help quell the Indian fighting. Fillmore owned considerable property in the downtown area. The house, at 1401 Curtis Street, was later sold to David H. Moffat, mining man, banker, and railroad builder. Moffat had already built his magnificent house across the street from this property, adjacent to the old W.B. Daniels house, at the northeast corner of

Fourteenth and Curtis streets. The Fillmore and Moffat houses were of the typical Victorian style. They were grand and large and were regarded as two of the finest homes in the city.

As the residential district moved away from downtown to Capitol Hill and elsewhere, the two houses were turned into rooming houses, with storefronts built onto the facades at street level. This was indicative of the fate of many of the old houses in the area. The Fillmore and Moffat houses were both wrecked in the 1920s.

The George Clayton residence was one of the early mansions to be wrecked. Clayton had made a fortune in real estate in Denver and elsewhere. Located at 1307 Tremont Place, the fifteen-room house, built in the French Second Empire style, was a study in Victorian excess, with a sloping mansard roof, many bay windows, a wrap-around porch embellished with the usual gingerbread decorations, and a fancy iron fence wrapped around the grounds. It was torn down in 1924 about the same time as the home of Amos Steck, at 1308 Glenarm Place. When it was constructed in 1884, the Steck house was considered one of the finest homes in the city. The fireplace mantels were imported, and the stairways throughout the house were made of solid walnut. Steck was postmaster in 1859 and later served as Denver mayor. He was also a member of the state legislature.

The 1920s and 1930s brought a surge of building in the downtown area, and the last remaining vestiges of residential life met with the wrecking ball. The home of Nathaniel Hill was a case in point. Hill, a U.S. senator from Colorado, built a fine house at Fourteenth and Welton streets, where he and his wife entertained the elite of the day in lavish style. The house, built in 1884 in the French Second Empire style, was complete with the standard order of rooms: drawing room, dining room, sitting room, and conservatory. Hill was the master of a social regime that was passed on to his daughter-in-law, Mrs. Crawford Hill. Those who walked through the massive mahogany doors of the Hill house on Fourteenth Street were top city leaders, socialites, and national political figures. When the Hills' daughters were of age to enter society, a large ballroom was added to the house to entertain their young peers and suitors.

When the Hills passed away, their children had married and established their own homes away from downtown. The house stood vacant for many years. When the Community Chest, a charitable organization that was a forerunner of the Denver United Way, was formed, the Hill mansion became its headquarters, and an addition was built to store Red Cross supplies. As the organization grew, more space was needed, and the mansion was abandoned for new quarters at the former L'Imperiale Hotel, farther east at Fourteenth Street and Court Place. By the 1930s, there was little use for a Victorian mansion in the depths of the business district, and the house was torn down in 1934 to make way for a gas station. The former mansions of David Moffat, John Evans, John Routt, mercantile prince John Sidney Brown, his brother Junius Brown, and T.H. Gray, all once lining Fourteenth Street, were already long gone. All through the 1920s and 1930s, private homes, large and small, throughout the entire downtown area were destroyed to accommodate the ever-increasing demand for commercial space, particularly offices and parking lots. By the end of the 1950s, it was extremely rare to find a house south of Twentieth Street or north of Cherry Creek, although many residential hotels and apartment houses could still be found in the area. By the 1960s, most residents had moved away. Those who stayed were usually low-income or the down-and-out. Rents reflected this. Many dilapidated hotel rooms could be had for a dollar or less a day. As this particular situation became the norm, the desirability of downtown living, to most people, was lost.

James Archer laid the foundation for his grand house at the corner of Thirteenth and Welton streets in 1875. He was founder of the Denver City Water Company, the city's first organized water supply. The house was one of downtown's showplaces, boasting an expansive lawn dotted with iron lawn ornaments and surrounded by a stone wall. Archer lived in the house until his death in 1882, and his widow remained there for many years. It later became the Denver Municipal Dispensary, a forerunner of Colorado General Hospital. Archer's grave in Riverside Cemetery in north Denver is marked with a stone statue of Archer standing on a tall pedestal. The mansion was torn down in 1925.

Another pioneer living in the area was John H.P. Voorhies, a mining engineer from Silverton who settled permanently in Denver in 1885. Upon his death in 1915, his estate gave a large sum of money to the city of Denver for the construction of the Voorhies Memorial at the north end of Civic Center Park in memory of Voorhies and his wife. The Voorhies had lived across the street at 1425 Cleveland Place. The gateway, designed by the prominent firm of Fisher & Fisher, was built of sandstone and marble, with murals by Denver artist Allen True and a reflecting pond with bronze sea lions sculpted by Robert Garrison, who also was responsible for the pair of bronze mountain lions at the municipal building at Colfax Avenue and Sherman Street.

Chapter 2

THE EXPANSION OF DOWNTOWN

The downtown area grew outward from its meager beginnings along the banks of Cherry Creek where it met the Platte River. Gold was the lure, and many men took the bait. Moving to Colorado from all points around the country, they were greeted with a desolate landscape, many hardships, and an unforgiving climate. Early Denver was bleak and almost treeless, much like the areas still to be found on the plains east of the city. Some of these men mined the hills above Denver, while some moved farther west to the mining camps of Leadville and Cripple Creek. Some gave up and moved on to California.

The gold and silver mines gave a great boost to the economy of the state and helped to found the city of Denver. Along with prospectors came the merchants who would sell them their equipment, clothing, and food; the saddlers and horse traders who would furnish their transportation; and the saloon keepers who would provide their entertainment. The downtown area was never meant to be exclusively residential. Commercial enterprise always played an important part in the development of the area. Commerce spread throughout the downtown area as the population grew. The area expanded in the 1880s, and growth continued unabated for the next five decades. Buildings rose to accommodate the ever-increasing demands for goods and services, and as a result, those who lived in the area found it less and less to their liking. Residential property values declined as residents felt themselves squeezed out by the hustle, dirt, and noise that inevitably followed the expansion of business. They began looking for more suitable living arrangements away from the center of town. The capitalists who had at one time ensconced themselves in their fancy homes downtown were now searching for a different kind of neighborhood within which to reestablish themselves, among others of the same standing, in a neighborhood that was relatively untouched and would not be mistaken for anything other than strictly elite. They found this area to the east, on a crest overlooking downtown.

Chapter 3

CAPITOL HILL

Capitol Hill was virtually uninhabited in the early 1880s. In the short span of a decade, block after block of expensive and elegant homes rose up. By 1890, the neighborhood had gained the reputation as the exclusive section of Denver, bounded by Twentieth Avenue, Broadway, Sixth Avenue, and York Street, and particularly the area south of Colfax Avenue. The area was spoken of in superlatives. The wealthy denizens fought to keep this neighborhood as their own, away from the common and ordinary of everyday life. They desired to set themselves apart, to display to the rest of the city that they were worthy and extraordinary people. They demanded the finest in living accommodations, with an eye to staying close to their business interests downtown. Fine houses lined street after street of Capitol Hill, built on the money made from gold, silver, oil, and land. Grounds were kept manicured, noise was forbidden, and rules of etiquette and protocol were strictly adhered to. Unlike today's wealthy and free-wheeling sports figures and movie stars, the well-heeled Victorians found themselves trapped in an endless array of constrictive social customs. Any breach was duly noted, and to be ostracized from this tight-knit group was the same as a death sentence. A black sheep appeared here and there; the rebelliousness of youth was bound to lead to a few exploits and indiscretions that were hushed up with the quick passing of a C-note.

In the days before movies, radio, or television, Denver's wealthy were Denver's royalty. Their comings and goings were duly noted in

Denver Public Library Western History Collection

Grant Street in 1889.

every edition of every newspaper. Teas, luncheons, motor trips, cruises, marriages, births, divorces, deaths, and the occasional scandal were all fodder for the press, to the consternation of some of these families and to the delight of others. Lists of departures from and arrivals to the city were noted daily in the early newspapers, along with who was "receiving callers" and who was being entertained.

These men lived in a world of ambition, hard work and sweat, smoke and soot, and deals and lawsuits. While many made their fortunes in silver and gold mining, many expanded their business interests to include real estate, utilities, railroads, manufacturing, ranching, agriculture, and oil. They joined their cronies at the exclusive Denver Club on Seventeenth Street downtown, the Athletic Club, and any number of country clubs and sporting clubs that offered everything from polo and hunting to motoring and camping.

They kept their wives and families surrounded with velvet, mohair, leather, fur, crystal, and gilt.

Children's parties were often as restrained in manner as were those of the parents. These princes and princesses of commerce not only associated closely with each other, they often married into each other's families, thus extending the lineage and the money. The Boettcher and Humphreys families, among the most powerful and influential in the state, were related, as were the Cheesman and Evans families, among others. The unspoken rule was to "not marry outside your position."

The times were a study in contrasts; the age was defined by a rapid surge in technology and industrial growth. It was an age of electrification and motorization. Yet, morals, manners, and style of dress were copied from the Old-World European aristocrats, and the rules were strict and adhered to rigidly. Any breach was considered to be an affront. Many books of the day were written on etiquette to help guide the host and guest toward a genial (and stiff) relationship. Rules on table manners, calling cards, invitations, gesturing, bowing, opening and closing of doors, telephoning, and practically every

other movement known to man spewed forth from these books as if they were the last words of the Almighty.

The years 1890–1891 were pivotal in the effort to make Capitol Hill an elite neighborhood. Money from gold and silver mining poured out of the hills of Colorado at an astonishing rate. Giant stone castles went up on every corner almost every day, the next one bigger and grander than the last. The newspapers made great note of these new palaces and went into detail regarding not only how much they cost and what they looked like inside and out, but who the owners were and where the money came from. Working-class readers ate it up.

From the very start, Capitol Hill was many things to many people, but exclusive it was not. An article from the *Denver Times* of 1901 had this to say:

> For some time Capitol Hill has been growing too inclusive. It no longer implies the social leverage of a few years ago when you were either on it or not on it and "the Hill" was the stronghold of the "smart set." In the rapid growth of the city, the ordinary set has been allowed to build houses which neither "frowned" nor "smiled" in grandeur and, indeed, one can no longer tell just who you are by where you live. There is only one part of Denver that has the exclusive air of Fifth Avenue and that is Quality Hill. Grant Avenue and Corona Street and Sixth to Eleventh Avenues are the limitations set by the exclusive leaders of fashion.

Although Capitol Hill, from the very beginning, was meant to be the bastion of the wealthy and accomplished, this was offset by the very fact that land use was extremely varied. While the gargantuan mansions of the elite went up, apartment buildings, terraces, garages, and storefronts followed close behind.

By the turn of the century, things were in full swing, with new mansions rising almost daily. Social boundaries were being set in place, and the social season was being dictated by a handful of self-pro-

claimed leaders of society, not the least of which was Mrs. Crawford Hill, whose husband was the son of Nathaniel Hill, owner of the Argo Smelter and a U.S. senator. The pillared Hill palace at the corner of Tenth Avenue and Sherman Street, which still stands, was the center of much of the social activity of any importance at the time. An invitation to the Hill residence was treated as a command. Mrs. Hill, the former Louise Sneed and married to the son of Senator Nathaniel Hill, was head of the so-called "Sacred 36," Denver's answer to New York's "Four Hundred" of Caroline Astor fame. To be included in Mrs. Hill's inner circle was a coveted honor.

Sherman and Grant streets were the most exclusive residential avenues in the city, with East Colfax running a close third. In this sense, "exclusive" referred not only to one's financial bracket, but also to race, and even to religion. Capitol Hill, and Quality Hill especially, was the cloistered enclave of the upper-crust Protestants and Catholics. Grant was lined on both sides with great Victorian houses from Seventh Avenue all the way north to Twentieth Avenue, with the houses on Sherman Street stretching about the same distance. Although these houses were not on the same scale and opulence as those being built back East in Newport, Philadelphia, or New York, they were certainly grander than anything the people of Denver had ever seen.

Architecture was a heavy mix of styles, from Queen Anne and English Tudor to Spanish and Italian, Moorish, Gothic Revival, Romanesque, and Greek Revival. Many featured towers, turrets, and prominent dormers. Arched windows and bay windows were standard fare, as well as cut-glass and stained-glass windows, carved stonework, and wide verandas that sometimes ran the entire length of the house. Many of the properties were surrounded by elaborate wrought-iron fencing and gates, and yards were filled with iron and stone statuary, fountains, and other garden ornaments. Iron "widow's walks" were a prominent rooftop feature. Yards were kept in immaculate shape by a crew of private gardeners, and the houses functioned flawlessly, thanks to a retinue of hired help. This left the master of the house with no domestic concerns and the lady of the house to her social and civic pursuits, unencumbered.

Grant Street as it appears today.

The accumulation of wealth did not guarantee the cultivation of good taste, however. Some of these houses were designed in a mishmash of styles, and it was difficult to tell where one stopped and another began. Some were ridiculously overbearing in their bid for attention. Style was not the ultimate factor, obviously. Size mattered. The bigger and grander, the better. Only those builders who were secure in their position opted for a more subdued effect.

A huge impact on the construction of mansions in Denver was the Panic of 1893, when the federal government went off the silver standard. Many fortunes were lost suddenly, and home construction plans were either put on hold or shelved altogether. Those who were able to recoup built their residences in a fashionable, yet much more restrained, manner. Carefree opulence gave way to measured restraint and sensibility.

Capitol Hill began losing its mansions early on, due to the impact of commerce and a widening of land usage in the area. Some houses were wrecked as early as 1910, and there was a surge of demolition in the 1920s with the popularity of the automobile. Travel away from the center of the city was now faster and easier. Places that were once considered "out in the country," such as Cherry Hills and the Country Club District, were now attracting residents away from Capitol Hill.

The 1960s were particularly damaging. Urban renewal, which was instituted to help solve the problem of downtown's growing blight, also reached into the depths of Capitol Hill. Property owners were more than happy to rid themselves of their white elephants, especially if a reasonable offer was tossed their way. The sites became high-rise offices, hotels, retail shops, and parking lots—many, many parking lots.

It wasn't until years later that the surviving mansions were salvaged and converted for use as medical and law offices, lofts, and condos. The idea finally came of age. It is common today to see vintage houses and other buildings used for modern purposes—a perfect blending of past and present.

Chapter 4

NORTH CAPITOL HILL

North Capitol Hill suffered much the same fate as its southern counterpart. Typical of the residences in the north section of Capitol Hill was the Craig house, at the southwest corner of East Sixteenth Avenue and Sherman Street. Alexander Crawford Craig came to Denver in 1876 from Missouri and opened a wholesale dry-goods business in downtown Denver. He first lived at 1920 California Street, the present site of the Church of the Holy Ghost. He built his new house on Sherman Street in 1885. Frank Edbrooke was the architect. As Craig expanded his dry-goods business, he also became heavily involved in real-estate development. He developed the A.C. Craig subdivision, East Pueblo Heights in Pueblo, Colorado, and a large tract of land in San Antonio, Texas. He also built the first summer home at Craig's Point at Grand Lake, later to become a desirable resort area, and founded the town of Craig, Colorado.

His only son, William Craig, became a prominent physician. Dr. Craig lived in the Sherman Street house from 1885 until his death in 1930. He was professor of surgery at the University of Colorado Medical School for forty-five years. He opened an office out of his house in 1893.

The house was a gathering place for professionals of the day: doctors, attorneys, and others who were friends of the Craigs. William Craig's wife, Bessie, daughter of a Confederate colonel, was a gracious and sought-out hostess.

The Charles Spalding Thomas house at 1609 Sherman Street.

A large Tiffany stained-glass window was prominent in the stairwell. The kitchen was as large as that of some hotels and was fitted with the latest conveniences.

Mrs. William Craig, the doctor's widow, closed the house in 1936, and it passed into the hands of her grandson, A. Crawford Craig, upon her death in 1938. In 1940, the residence was converted to a rooming house and remained so until it was sold and torn down in 1952 to make way for the Farmer's Union Building. A great oak mantelpiece from the drawing room, and a large stained-glass window were given to the Central City Opera House Association.

The Charles Spalding Thomas house was also typical of the style of residences in this part of Capitol Hill. Thomas, who served as Colorado's governor from 1899 to 1901 and as U.S. senator from 1912 to 1921, built this rambling Victorian pile at 1609 Sherman Street in the 1880s. The scene of elaborate parties and other social functions, the house was

subsequently leased to Frank Hearne. Hearne was a director of the Colorado Fuel & Iron Company and was involved in Gould/Rockefeller interests. Hearne lived in the house a short while and soon purchased the former Donald Fletcher mansion at the southwest corner of Sixteenth and Grant Street. When Hearne vacated the Sherman Street house, the property reverted back to the Thomases.

Charles Thomas was also a lawyer and a businessman. Born in Georgia in 1849, he studied law at the University of Michigan and moved to Colorado after his graduation. He practiced law in Denver and was city attorney from 1875 to 1876. After a brief partnership with Senator Thomas Patterson, Thomas formed the law offices of Thomas, Bryant, Makburn & Nye. The company's specialty was mining litigation, conducted during the turbulent years of mining in Colorado. Many problems arose in the state's fledgling industry, and many lawyers such as Charles Thomas made considerable money settling disputes between management and labor and deal-

Built for Peter Gottesleben, an early merchant, this mansion at 1901 Sherman Street later became offices.

ing with the question of property rights. Thomas and his wife, Emma, were social leaders in the city at the turn of the century.

The Thomas mansion was originally two stories high but was later enlarged to three. A wing was added to the west side of the house in about 1892, giving the house a total of about thirty rooms. Adhering to the fashion of the day, many cut-glass and stained-glass windows were found throughout the house, and the heavy wood paneling, archways, stairwells, and hardwood flooring gave the interior a rich appearance. The house was filled with valuable antiques acquired by the Thomases during their travels. When Charles Thomas died, the property went to his daughter, Edith. She lived for many years in a twelve-room apartment on the second floor, while the rest of the home was rented to paying guests.

As commercial space in the area became more desirable, the many residences, most of which had become boardinghouses or schools, or were vacant, started to come down. The Thomas house was wrecked in the spring of 1960 to make way for a parking lot, and the property is still used in that capacity.

In the late nineteenth century, practically the entire neighborhood north of the State Capitol building, from Broadway to Grant and Colfax Avenue to Twentieth Avenue was filled with similar houses. They started to come down as early as the 1910s, and they were replaced by office buildings, garages, apartments, and storefronts as commerce spread outward from downtown. By the 1970s, only a few remnants remained, most notably the George Schleier house at 1665 Grant and the towered long gallery, once part of the Donald Fletcher estate, at 1575 Grant, which was long used as the headquarters of the Knights of Columbus.

Two important houses in the area came down in the 1920s to make way for the Grosvenor Arms

apartment building: that of Charles Dickenson, at 1605 Logan Street, and Dr. Charles Denison, just north, at 1623 Logan Street. Both were built on a large scale, designed by architect William Lang in collaboration with his partner, Marshall Pugh. The Dickenson house was particularly exuberant, with rusticated stone (a Lang trademark), a rounded three-story tower, tall chimneys, stained-glass windows, and a wraparound porch.

The Peter Gottesleben residence, once located at 1901 Sherman Street, was one of Denver's finest

mansions when it was built in 1889. The solid construction and masterful stone carvings gave it an imposing air. Gottesleben came to the United States from his native Germany at the behest of his brother, who had followed the lure of gold in the 1850s. Gottesleben was one of the city's most successful early merchants, dealing in jewelry and other businesses in the downtown area. He and his family operated Gottesleben & Sons, located at 1104 Sixteenth Street, at the turn of the century. Peter Gottesleben died in 1919, and his descendants remained in the house for the next thirty years.

This residence at 1540 Sherman Street, now demolished, was typical of the many meticulously designed mansions in the North Capitol Hill area.

Denver Public Library Western History Collection

1648 Washington Street. Designed by architect William Lang, this large house still stands, along with two townhouses, also designed by Lang, at 1624 and 1628 Washington.

The house, constructed of rusticated stone, was set on four lots, surrounded by a low retaining wall topped with decorative iron scrollwork. The exterior boasted a large turret, cut-glass and leaded-glass windows, and a pillared, arched entryway. The interior featured plastered and stenciled ceilings, mosaic tile floors, and cut-glass chandeliers complete with candles, gas jets, and electric fittings.

The mansion was converted to office use in 1953 and was torn down in the 1960s. A high-rise office building occupies the space today.

The Richard Pearce mansion, built in the 1890s at 1712 Sherman Street, was a Denver landmark for decades. Pearce was a metallurgist and mining expert who invented a process to separate metals from ore. The twenty-room house was a masterpiece of design and craftsmanship. Many of the rooms had hand-carved fireplaces, all of different design. The mansion was entirely surrounded by a high wall of brick and wrought iron.

In the 1920s, the house became the Democratic Club, which was used for meetings and musicales. For a time, the house held music and art studios. A popular restaurant, the Casa Rosa de Oro, was added to the main floor. It became a rooming house for a short time before being wrecked in the 1960s. The site is now occupied by a high-rise office building.

Chapter 5

WHEN COLFAX WAS "THE" AVENUE

A fact that has been lost to the last three or so generations is that East Colfax Avenue was once considered to be a very desirable address. The section running east from Broadway to York Street was, at one time, filled on both sides with large, expensive, exotic residences, interrupted by the occasional terrace, church, or shop.

Colfax was, in the beginning, a long, narrow dirt road that cut a direct path through town from east to west. The homes that rose on this avenue were on par with those of Quality Hill, and Colfax was known as the grand avenue of the era from 1890 to about 1910, when it started to lose its prestige. Commercial enterprise was moving in and forcing property owners out. During the early years, many city leaders built their houses here, including William Byers, owner and editor of the *Rocky Mountain News* in its earliest days. He built his house at 1500 Sherman Street. This home was torn down about 1920 to be replaced with a government building. Albert Welch's grand Victorian pile, with its towers and veranda, sat at Colfax Avenue and Grant Street, where the Argonaut Hotel now stands. Job A. Cooper, Colorado governor, lived at 1500 Grant Street, and Rodney Curtis, grocer and druggist, later to become a major organizer of the Denver Tramway System, kept a large house at the northwest corner of Colfax and Pennsylvania until his death in 1915. The mansion was later used by the Immaculate Conception Cathedral, located next door to the west. A small park, part of the cathedral, now occupies the site.

Otto Mears, the railroad man, had a great house at the southeast corner of Colfax and Washington, a site now occupied by the Argonaut Liquor store. Platt Rogers, a prominent attorney, built his spacious home at 1500 Washington Street, later the site of the Denver Clinic Building. Captain William Bethel built his French castle at 1156 East Colfax, next door to John W. Nesmith, who ran the Colorado Iron Works. The Bethel house was later the home of Senator Lawrence Phipps. Both were torn down to make way for the Colfax Indoor Market, which, in turn, was torn down to make way for the Heart of Denver Hotel.

As commerce expanded outward from the downtown area, and people became more mobile as the automobile took over the streets, Colfax became a business center rather than a place to live, although many comfortable apartment buildings still dotted the area. Most of the houses were converted to commercial use or were torn down. Some are still visible behind their quickly built storefronts, such as the George Williamson residence, at 1600 East Colfax, and the mansion at the northwest corner of Colfax and Marion, which has served as a retail store, a bar, and, most recently, the Janleone Restaurant.

Ed Chase built his dream house at the southeast corner of Colfax and Race Street. With a sweep of seventy feet facing Colfax Avenue, his was but one of the many palatial residences that made the avenue a most desirable place to live among the elite of the city in the late Nineteenth Century. The house was built in the Queen Anne style—so popular in that era—of dark red brick and a large corner tower with a rounded dome. Many of the houses in the immediate area were built in the same fashion. Ed Chase was hardly in the same class as his neighbors, however. When he died in 1921 at the age of eighty-three, he had become many things to many people. Some regarded him as an elegantly dressed capitalist and entrepreneur who drove a fine car, wore expensive clothes, and smiled benevolently at the neighborhood children. Others saw him as a crass upstart, with questionable early beginnings and a less-than-honorable income. There was no doubt that he made himself into the region's gambling kingpin.

Although Chase had an arrest record and was sometimes vilified by the public and the press, he learned to skate around the police and was able to attend to his various illicit concerns with little interference, for the most part, and even gained a modicum of respectability. He became a benefactor of sorts to those around him who were in need. When he came to the city as a young man in the 1860s, he established the Palace Theater on Blake Street in lower downtown. The theater offered clever entertainment, something new to the dusty city of Denver. Fast-paced vaudeville and famous personalities of the day brought throngs of patrons to this house of amusement. Chase capitalized on this success and soon expanded his interests. He acquired the Arcade Club and also the Inter-Ocean Club, which was the former residence of William B. Daniels, department store tycoon, located at 1422 Curtis Street.

The house that Chase built on Race Street was torn down in 1926 to make way for the new Aladdin Theater, which was to be Denver's premiere neighborhood theater for the next six decades. Built by Harry Huffman, Denver theater operator, the four-story showplace was built in the style of the Arabian Nights. The exterior was modeled after the Taj Mahal, and the interior was like walking into a dream. The theatergoing public was held in awe at what they found inside: thick carpets in jade green, big plush seats, an expansive ceiling painted in sky blue with hundreds of tiny, twinkling lights that looked like stars when the house lights were turned down, a completely equipped nursery, a waiting room, and a smoking lounge. They found exotic Arabian murals and decorations, and even a fountain. Despite its longtime success, by the late 1970s, revenue started to slide, in spite of first-run showings. By 1984, the theater was up for sale. City council gave the okay to level the theater for a planned retail and condo complex, but nothing ever came of that. After a few meek attempts to find a use for the building, including a restaurant and nightclub, the Aladdin was torn down in August 1984 to make way for a Walgreen's Drugstore. There is little nowadays to tell of either this motion-picture palace or the palace built by slot machines.

Denver Municipal Facts

This residence at 1509 Vine Street, built for R. Quigley and subsequently owned by prominent attorney Tyson Dines, became a music conservatory before being torn down in 1930 to make way for the Leetonia Apartments.

Little is known about one of the most impressive houses along this stretch of Colfax: the Adolph Gustofsen castle, a huge dwelling constructed in 1890 at the southeast corner of Colfax Avenue and Gilpin Street. The overblown castle, built of rusticated stone, featured cut-glass, plate-glass, and stained-glass windows; towers and open balconies; a red slate roof; and other interesting architectural elements. The interior was finished with different hardwoods,

including oak and mahogany. The house boasted hot-water heat and full electric service—an innovation of the time. The house changed hands a number of times and for a while sat empty, generating rumors of ghostly apparitions. Neighborhood children crossed the street to avoid going too close to the house.

In October 1933, the house was wrecked to make way for the O'Meara-Young Motor Company, and the site was later used for the McCarty-Sherman car sales lot. The original showroom is now the Camy Food Market.

Platt Rogers, a prominent Denver attorney, built his Colfax residence early on, before the avenue acquired its air of distinction. Rogers had constructed a simple but roomy house at 1500 Washington Street, set back from the street, with a sweeping lawn extending to Colfax. Rogers was the city's first judge of the criminal division of district court and was elected mayor in 1901. While in office, he was greatly responsible for the planning and construction of the Civic Center complex and the Sixteenth Street viaduct. The Rogers house was the center of the social scene at the time it was built in the 1880s. His daughter, Margaret, was married there to Senator Lawrence Phipps.

The long-gone Adolph Gustofsen castle at 1470 Gilpin Street was allegedly haunted.

Denver Public Library Western History Collection

Platt Rogers built his country house in the 1880s when Colfax was indeed a country road.

Eventually, the house was expanded to twenty-two rooms. The living room, with its French doors, opened out onto the terrace facing Colfax. In the winters, this lawn was flooded for ice-skating parties, popular with Rogers' guests. The dining room occupied an entire wing of its own and could seat fifty guests comfortably. The main floor also contained a library, a kitchen, and a pantry. Upstairs were ten bedrooms and six baths. Along the back of the residence were the large stables, later used for automobiles, which also held living quarters for the staff. The terrace, originally open to the street, was eventually walled in as a barrier from the increasing noise from Colfax.

Platt Rogers died in 1928, and his widow lived on in the house with her staff. The noise drove her out, and she settled in the country-club area. The Colfax house was converted to a boardinghouse. The high wall surrounding the property was torn down, and

the gardens were dug up and paved over for use as a parking lot for a used-car lot. By the late 1940s, the mansion found an unlikely use as a restaurant, first as the Casa Rosa de Oro, which was formerly located in the Richard Pearce mansion at 1712 Sherman Street (then being run as the Democratic Club); then later as a seafood specialty restaurant. Parking for the restaurant fronted Colfax on the old used car lot. In the mid-1950s, the restaurant abandoned the house, and in 1957, the house was wrecked to make way for a new medical complex, named the Denver Clinic, headed by Dr. Frank McGlone, prominent physician. Today, the building houses offices for the Colorado Aids Project, and an adjacent building to the north is the Denver Police Department, District 6.

Platt Rogers' daughter, Margaret, and her husband, Lawrence C. Phipps, lived in the former William Bethel chateau at the corner of Marion and Colfax in the early 1900s. The mansion was one of the city's showplaces and became a center of Denver's social scene early on. An article from the *Denver Republican* of 1894 highlighted one of the parties given by Captain and Mrs. Bethel for Denver's "Top Drawer:"

Naturally the interest of the week from society's point of view centered in the reception and ball given Thursday afternoon and evening in the magnificent residence of Captain W. D. Bethel of Colfax avenue. Externally this immense residence presents the appearance of a French chateau, and the internal appointments are the most superb in Denver.

And on Thursday evening an observor might well have imagined himself gazing upon the gorgeous panorama of a court ball. Eight hundred invitations were issued for reception and ball jointly, and at 5 p.m. the carriages began pulling into the portcochere.

The vast hall with its ceilings of blue from which hundreds of electric lights flashed, was itself like an immense conservatory with its palms and ferns. Its hundreds of flowering plants and graceful vines. But the crowning beauty of the decorations was the roses. Roses in rare costly vases, in priceless crystal bowls, roses in banks and mounds where-to cupids might well be tempted to deport themselves, and roses apparently rooted beneath the polished oaken floor, and twining themselves in and out among the carved woodwork of hall and dining room, music and breakfast room, library and boudoir, a tribute of sweet incense to the beauty and brilliance thronging everywhere.

The orchestra was stationed back of a broad portiere woven of smilax. Doorways were wreathed with smilax and heavy robes of smilax studded with gem-like blossoms of vivid hue concealed mouldings and window casings. The broad staircase from the reception hall to the upper rooms

on the third floor seemed like an avenue bordered with stately palms and flowering shrubs. Here the receiving party stood. Mrs. Bethell wore a heavy white moire combined with heliotrope velvet, with garniture of point lace, and carried English violets. Mrs. Foster wore a bodice of white and gold brocade with skirt of buttercup satin and carried red roses. Mrs. Edrington's costume was of yellow brocade and satin profusely trimmed with point lace, and her corsage was nearly covered by the immense branch of American beauties. Inasmuch as there were 700 guests present it would be a fruitless task to try to describe the extensive costumes seen. More than a few Paris gowns were worn.

The refreshment tables were spread in four upper rooms and they feasted every sense. Soft strains of music floated in through the open doors while the wealth of flowers dispated the palm of beauty with the rich table service of cut glass, crystal, silver and china. Apparently every delicacy that could tempt the palate was there and champagne sparkled in numberless costly glasses.

Another example of an early Colfax mansion was that of Job Cooper, at 1500 Grant Street, adjacent to the State Capitol Building. Cooper was born in Illinois in 1843. He studied law at Knox College and was admitted to the bar in 1867. After he moved to Denver in 1872, he became a partner of A.C. Phelps and later gained a position with the German Bank. He was also briefly involved in the cattle industry. Cooper had a wide range of business interests, including finance, mining, and land speculation. He built the Cooper Building in 1891 at Seventeenth and Curtis streets, a downtown landmark for decades. It was widely praised as one of the finest buildings of its kind in the West.

Cooper, a staunch Republican, was active in local politics and was elected Colorado governor in 1889, succeeding Alva Adams and beating Democratic opponent Thomas Patterson, who was the editor and principal owner of the *Rocky Mountain News.* Cooper

The Job Cooper mansion, at the northeast corner of Colfax Avenue and Grant Street, adjacent to the State Capitol, when that building was ringed by stately houses.

served as governor until 1891. Afterwards, he became president of the National Bank of Commerce and went into semiretirement in 1897. He devoted his remaining years to his investments in mining and real estate.

Cooper's house was built in the late 1870s, and a number of additions were constructed over the years. After Cooper died in 1899, the house had several subsequent owners. By the early 1900s, city council had legalized commercial zoning for Colfax Avenue, and the formerly elite residential area saw a great depreciation in property values. Many of the home owners moved away from Colfax. These former monuments to the rich fell into disrepair and were allowed to sit vacant and unattended. Some were turned into apartments or rooming houses, and many were demolished. The Cooper house was gone by the late 1920s, and for a while the property was an empty lot. [In 1930, lumberman Hugh M. Woods built his new house at 75 Ash Street in east Denver and included in the construction not only a fireplace and other elements taken from the Cooper house, but also from old East High School downtown. The rough rock on the exterior of the home and the slate on the roof were both used in the original school building, which was razed in the early 1920s when a new East High School was opened at Colfax and Detroit.]

In the following decade, a filling station was built on the site. The business changed hands a number of times, and the property was finally sold in the mid-1970s for construction of the new Silver State Savings and Loan. The building has been used by the Colorado Education Association for the past several years.

One very visible survivor is the Henry Bohm house, built in 1896 at Colfax Avenue and High Street. Although the structure has always attracted its share of attention, it's hard to consider that this was, at one time, a private residence. It has the appearance of always having been a multifamily dwelling due to the additions that have been made to the original structure.

Bohm was a pioneer in the city's jewelry business. Born in New York in 1846, he moved to Kansas City at the age of twenty-eight and opened his first jewelry store there. He later came to Colorado, where he settled in Leadville. After about a year there, he moved to Denver, where he opened a jewelry store at Sixteenth and Arapahoe streets. This business later became the Bohm-Allen Company. The store operated at that location for almost forty years, until Bohm's retirement in 1919.

While the Bohms were in residence at the High Street house, Baron Walter Von Richtofen, who planned the Montclair District in east Denver and built his namesake castle there, died and laid in state in this house prior to his burial in 1898.

Henry Bohm sold the house in 1899 and moved to 1655 Sherman. He moved to 1040 Pennsylvania about 1905 and died there in 1920.

The High Street house was sold in 1912, this time to Noah Hayden Griffith, grandfather of the current owner, Margot Crowe, and is operated today as the Holiday Chalet Bed and Breakfast, the only three-diamond inn on Colfax in Denver. Noah Griffith purchased the property as an investment. He died

The Henry Bohm house at the southwest corner of Colfax Avenue and High Street.

Author's Collection

This outstanding stained-glass window was moved from the south side of the house to the north side during the remodeling of the 1920s.

during the flu epidemic of 1918, and his wife, Ida, converted the house into twelve efficiency apartments. Aside from her new-found role as a landlady, she focused on her hobby of china painting, which was a popular pastime of the day. She was unique in the fact that all of her patterns were hers alone, while most other women followed those supplied by companies or catalogs. She kept a kiln in the basement of the house. Examples of her painted china are on display. One outstanding pattern has a children's motif. Reproductions of her work can be purchased.

Margot Crowe's parents took over the house in 1952. High taxes demanded that the family increase their revenue, and the house was converted to an apartment-hotel. Since its conversion, the hotel has attracted visitors from all over the globe. Mrs. Crowe took over the management in 1985 and has maintained the Old World ambiance of the hotel, while, at the same time, keeping up-to-date with the changes Colfax has seen in the past few decades. Slightly different in character than its bed-and-breakfast cousins that populate the neighborhood, the hotel has a feel of something long ago; crystal chandeliers and old lace keep the fantasy alive. The fact that it has remained in the same family for more than ninety years may also have something to do with it.

The entrance to the Holiday Chalet originally faced High Street, and was numbered 1475. It was changed later to the Colfax side, when Ida Griffith

made a number of additions to the house to convert it to apartment use. The twin sunporches to the east and an extension to the west were added in the early 1920s. The house has many outstanding features, such as large, decorative stained-glass windows and generously proportioned rooms. The dark pink exterior has a commanding presence, with tall chimneys and fancy parapets.

The entrance from Colfax Avenue opens into an odd floor plan, due to the many remodelings over the years. A long, narrow hallway, with guest rooms off both sides, stretches to the breakfast room at the opposite end of the house. The hall is lined with Ida Griffith's artwork and a number of family portraits. This narrowness belies the open feeling one gets due to the many sunporches. There are nine guest rooms on three floors. The rooms are decorated in an attractive Victorian theme, and all have their own kitchens. There is also a tea room on the main floor, once Ida Griffith's apartment.

As the Inglenook Apartments, it survived the harsh days of the Depression and has come into its own as an outstanding example of a family-run business in the heart of Capitol Hill. "We get quite a wide variety of people from all over the world," said Mrs. Crowe, "and we wouldn't have it any other way."

She also commented on the ups and downs of running a business on Colfax Avenue. "They are in the planning stages, right now, of yet another revitalization program [Blueprint Colfax, a long-range concept for Colfax Avenue from Broadway to York Street], one that I think will work. While other such plans have never had much of an impact, this one is backed by a number of politically connected advisors. I may not see it in my lifetime, but I have no doubt it will happen. In the meantime, Colfax continues to be a vital part of the community."

Colfax, since becoming part of U.S. Highway 40, has been heavily traveled. It is a destination for shoppers and continues to be, reputedly, the longest commercial street in the nation, cutting a path directly through the center of the city from Golden all the way east beyond the former Fitzsimmons Army Hospital.

Chapter 6

JOHN GOOD HOUSE

1007 PENNSYLVANIA STREET

ARCHITECT: ISAAC HODGSON

BUILT: 1890

One of the most widely known and elaborate mansions in all of Capitol Hill was that built for John A. McMurtrie at the northwest corner of Tenth and Pennsylvania streets. McMurtrie was the chief engineer for the Denver & Rio Grande Railroad when it built its Royal Gorge line and was later the chief engineer for the Southern Pacific Railroad. He came to Denver in 1871 from Pennsylvania and went to work for D.C. Dodge, general manager of the Denver & Rio Grande Railroad, as chief engineer. McMurtrie was responsible for the construction of some of the most difficult aspects of laying out the growing railroad system in the state. He built the McMurtrie Building, located at Sixteenth Street and Cleveland Place, one of the first completely fireproof buildings in the city. It was later purchased by Charles Kountze and Dennis Sheedy, prominent local investors. McMurtrie was involved in real estate throughout the city and in numerous other business affairs.

When McMurtrie died in 1899, the family sold the house to Dr. J.W. Graham, prospector and one-time partner in the famous Little Jonny Mine in Leadville. Graham only held the property for a short time before selling it to John Good, the man who became most closely associated with the house. Good had amassed a fortune in mining and railroads and through his investments in the Tivoli Brewery. He also was involved in real estate and banking matters and was one of the organizers of the German Bank, later the German National Bank. He came to Denver in 1859 and built one of the

first commercial stores in the city. He established the Rocky Mountain Brewing Company, the first brewery in Denver, which was later bought out by the Zang Brewing Company. Good was twice city treasurer. He and his wife Rosalia were not members of the Denver social set, but they did host many parties in their Pennsylvania Street mansion. They were known as much for their warmth and humor as they were for their many charitable efforts throughout the city. Mrs. Good was known for her vivacious personality and her warmth of character. She traveled extensively, drove her automobiles at top speed, and loved to entertain. The house was always open and was usually filled with friends and relatives.

The house was constructed of red Colorado sandstone and had a red tile roof. The property covered sixty feet on Pennsylvania and one hundred feet along Tenth Avenue. Massive entrance doors with intricate bronze and wrought ironwork opened into a maze of rooms, hallways, and corridors. Hand-carved paneling and other exotic woodwork was found throughout the house, and the many fireplaces were of carved marble. The main floor had a solid oak inlay. The Rose Room had a plaster ceiling that was compared to ivory, with elaborate designs, and rose-design wallpaper covered the walls. Every room in the mansion was finished in a different color. To the north of the house was a sprawling garden area that connected the house to the large stables, later used as a garage.

Amidst all of this splendor, tragedy struck more than once. Of the Good's six children, four died after moving into the Pennsylvania Street house. John Good died in 1918. A fifth son, John Edward Good, a well-known sportsman and socialite who took over his father's vast business interests, died suddenly in 1931. Only Mrs. Good and a daughter survived, and they remained together in the huge house until the daughter's marriage. Mrs. Good then lived in the house alone, except for a small faithful staff to look after her. She died in 1936, well into her nineties.

The mansion stood vacant for a period until it was sold to Forrest Goody in 1941. He opened the house as the Castle Leigh Guest Home, a rooming

house for college-age men. While numerous changes were made to the interior to accommodate the new clientele—as many as sixty at one time—the outside remained the same. By the late 1950s, the property had become increasingly expensive to maintain and was put up for sale. There were no interested buyers.

John Good's castle, one of the most elaborate of all of Denver's mansions, in the middle of Quality Hill.

Like so many other Capitol Hill palaces, there were not many uses for such a place. Vague plans to operate the house as a fancy restaurant fell through. It continued to serve paying tenants until the property was again sold. The house was wrecked in 1965. An apartment building occupies the site today.

27

Chapter 7

DAVID H. MOFFAT HOUSE

808 GRANT STREET

ARCHITECT: HARRY MANNING

BUILT: 1910–11

David H. Moffat's story is indicative of the drive and ambition that made the pioneers of Colorado great. Born in Washingtonville, New York, in 1839, he went to work at a young age in the banking business. Through his diligence, he was soon promoted to assistant teller. He was only sixteen years old. He was soon summoned by his brother to Des Moines, Iowa, and went to work for a new bank there. Soon after, he was invited to join another bank in Omaha, Nebraska, and was made head cashier. This was the same time when news was circulating about the discovery of gold in the Pike's Peak Region of Colorado. David Moffat soon found himself headed west.

After he arrived in Denver in 1859, Moffat immediately opened a book and stationery store with a partner, C.C. Woolworth. The new store was located at Eleventh and Larimer streets, south of Cherry Creek. Business flourished, and Moffat was invited to join the First National Bank of Denver as a cashier. He was eventually elected its president. He always had an interest in railroads, however, and in 1869, he made a proposal to a group of capitalists to build a line from Denver to Cheyenne, Wyoming. The plan was executed, and the line connected with Union Pacific. Denver was now effectively on a main railroad line. Moffat soon expanded his railroad interests to include lines to several mining camps, including Cripple Creek. At one time or another, Moffat was associated with almost all the major businessmen of his day, including Eben Smith, Governor John Evans, General William Palmer, Granville Dodge, and Walter S. Cheesman.

For a time, David Moffat lived in this rambling mansion at the northeast corner of Seventeenth and Lincoln streets, now the site of the United Bank Building.

He shrewdly invested in mining properties, investments that were to bring him vast wealth. He had a major stake in the fabulously rich Little Pittsburgh Mine and the famous Anaconda mines, among many others. Not content to rest on his laurels, he soon formulated a plan to run a rail line directly through the Rocky Mountains to connect Denver with Salt Lake City, considered, at the time, to be an almost impossible feat. The Moffat Road Company was formed by Moffat and a group of businessmen, and plans for the line went ahead, although construction took many years. Moffat did not live to see his dream come true. After having made some very expensive financial blunders, he died in New York in 1911, practically bankrupt, while trying to raise capital for the Moffat Road. The Moffat Road and Tunnel did not open for transcontinental rail travel until 1927.

Moffat purchased property at Eighth Avenue and Grant Street in 1904, and in 1910, he started construction of a massive, thirty-six-room mansion. Impressively situated on a hill, the huge house boasted a large reception room that had a chandelier with 4,000 hand-cut crystals, especially made for Moffat. The oval dining room was furnished entirely in blue and could seat fifty guests comfortably. There were also a music room and a sitting room, and a master suite and library on the second floor. The finely carved staircase featured a three-panel Tiffany stained-glass window on the landing. Moffat ordered it at a cost of $25,000. Moffat and his wife had planned this house while living in a huge Victorian pile at the northeast corner of Seventeenth and Lincoln streets, now the site of the United Bank Building.

When Moffat died, his widow held onto the house a few years, living mainly on the second floor to keep expenses down. She eventually sold the property and moved into an apartment in her former house on Lincoln Street.

The new owner was Bessie Cosgriff, widow of J.B. Cosgriff, who had made a fortune in banking and cattle and sheep ranching. Cosgriff was a major force behind the construction of Union Station and was a president of Hamilton National Bank. Mrs. Cosgriff became widely known as one of the city's most gracious hostesses, and the mansion became the center of social activity in Capitol Hill. Mrs. Cosgriff lived in the mansion until 1938, when it was again sold, this time to the Order of Ahepa, or the American Hellenic Education Progressive Association, Chapter 145, a Greek fraternal order devoted to Americanization classes and lectures on government and business. Mrs. Cosgriff's son, J.W. Cosgriff, James Dikeou, and Panayes Dikeou were among those who negotiated the sale.

By the late 1960s, plans were made to demolish the mansion for a modern office building, a plan that brought about a firestorm of protest from preservation groups and private citizens. The previous decade had been harsh for the vintage and historic structures in and around Capitol Hill, and a vast amount had already been bulldozed. Many others were threatened with destruction. The Landmark Preservation Committee of Denver designated the Moffat mansion for preservation, along with the D & F tower downtown, the Denver Women's Press Club at 1325 Logan Street, and Four Mile House in east Denver. This plan was fought by the owners of the mansion. The Denver Planning Board allied itself with the preservationists, and a court order by the city brought a delay in demolition. Historic Denver, Inc., which was formed a few years earlier to save the Molly Brown house from a similar fate, tried to purchase the Moffat mansion. There were plans and suggestions by many as to what to do with the house, but, despite the best efforts of those in-

Constructed at the top of a sloping site, the Moffat mansion at Eighth Avenue and Grant Street was built to impress.

Denver Public Library Western History Collection

The huge Tiffany stained-glass window at the stairway landing, a centerpiece of the Moffat mansion, was later removed to a new office building on the same site.

volved, plans for demolition went ahead. In 1972, an auction was held to sell all remaining furnishings and fixtures in the house. The mansion was wrecked that same year.

A new office building was constructed on the site, and the Tiffany window that previously had graced the landing of the mansion was installed above the entrance to the office building. It was eventually sold and removed. The great stone urns that stood at either side of the main entrance to the mansion were moved to the front of Denver House, an apartment building at 1055 Logan Street, where they remain today. Ahepa is still listed as active, with offices in south Denver.

Chapter 8

JOHN CAMPION HOUSE

800 LOGAN STREET

ARCHITECTS: AARON GOVE & THOMAS WALSH

BUILT: 1896

I n the early 1960s, one of Denver's most celebrated homes sat empty, dark, vandalized, and strewn with trash and dead birds. This was the former home of John Campion, mining tycoon and empire builder who was known and revered throughout the state. Born in Canada in 1848, he soon moved with his parents and siblings to California, where his father had found work. He was sent back to school at his birthplace, along with his brother, to continue his education. The boys, however, had other ideas and ran away from school to enlist in the navy. John was accepted, while his brother was rejected and returned to school. When his enlistment was up, John joined his parents in Sacramento and took up the mining trade at the time of a major mine discovery. He rapidly advanced to management but very early on found himself in a reversal of fortune and lost practically everything he had made. He packed up his belongings and left for Eureka, Nevada, where he developed and sold numerous mining properties. Again he amassed a considerable amount of money. He became a major investor in the Pioche Phoenix silver mine, a venture that brought in an even larger fortune. He soon got news of a carbonate discovery in the Leadville, Colorado, area and was one of the first to invest in and develop those properties. Campion was also a pioneer in the sugar-beet industry, along with Charles Boettcher, and became a major investor in the Great Western Sugar Company.

He had interests in the Tabor Grand Opera block at Sixteenth and Curtis streets, and the Ideal Cement Company, in partnership

Ferril, Sketches of Colorado

John Francis Campion.

man of great personal fortune, Campion made plans to build a mansion befitting a man of his stature. He chose the northeast corner of Eighth Avenue and Logan Street in Denver's exclusive Capitol Hill neighborhood. He was already leasing a place nearby.

Campion married Nellie Daly, sister of Thomas Daly, president of the Capitol Life Insurance Company. During a previous trip to Europe with his wife, he had purchased thousands of dollars worth of paintings, Persian carpets, statuary, and other art that would be used to decorate his new home.

The house was built in the solid Italian Renaissance style of Rawlins gray sandstone. It was four stories high with a full basement. The austere, impressive exterior featured stone columns and porches with tiled flooring. The roof was finished with red Spanish tiles.

with Boettcher, who was another enterprising Colorado pioneer. Campion was a principal owner of Leadville's Little Jonny Mine, a strike that brought untold wealth to others as well, including J.J. Brown, husband of Margaret "Molly" Brown of *Titanic* fame. The Little Jonny had been developed earlier and was thought to have run its course when Campion applied new technology, which included core drilling, to dig deeper than others had previously done. The deeper drilling resulted in the discovery of massive gold deposits that were among the largest in the world.

Campion was president of the Napite Mining Company in Breckenridge and vice-president of the Denver, Northwestern & Pacific Raliroad. He was a founder of the Museum of Natural History in City Park, now the Museum of Nature and Science, and his donated collection of gold specimens can still be viewed there. He was president of the Denver Chamber of Commerce at the turn of the century. Campion was also generous to the church.

He, along with Dennis Sheedy and J.J. Brown, was instrumental in the construction of the new Cathedral of the Immaculate Conception at Colfax Avenue and Logan Street. He also donated funds for the cathedral's bells and other improvements. Now a

The interior of the house was fit for a king, built of many exotic hardwoods and fitted with stained-glass and cut-glass windows, many imported. To the left of the main entrance was the Blue Room, essentially a sitting room. To the right was the library; farther down was a music room, finished in various hardwoods with oak flooring. The dining room, twenty by twenty-four feet, was adjacent to the large kitchen, the cook's pantry, the maid's pantry, the servants' dining area, and the back hall. These rooms opened into a large reception hall that was more than thirty feet in length, with its wide staircase leading to the rooms upstairs. The conservatory on the south side of the house, originally a wide, open porch, was paneled with dark, carved wood and was used alternately as a sunporch and a botanics room.

The second floor contained three bedrooms, an art room, a morning room, and two tiled bathrooms with large closets, all finished in various hardwoods. Also located on this floor were a nursery and playroom. Servants' quarters were located on the east side of this floor. Five more bedrooms were located on the third floor, along with two more baths and additional servants' quarters. The house also boasted a pool table in a game room that was nineteen by twenty-four feet, and a regulation-size bowling alley in the basement made of quartered oak. It was used

Denver Public Library Western History Collection

The Campion residence was one of Capitol Hill's true showplaces, built with mining money and before personal income taxes.

by the Campion children, grandchildren, and guests alike. The rear of the basement held a vegetable room, a gym, a large laundry, a boiler room, and a coal room. Coal was delivered by cart and loaded into the basement by means of a chute. Vendors also delivered vegetables and ice to the house.

The manicured grounds took up 125 feet on Eighth Avenue and 225 feet on Logan Street. A space of sixty-three feet to the north provided room for the stables, later used for automobiles. The top-floor ballroom was the scene of many well-publicized and

enviable parties and quickly became the social center of Capitol Hill.

When the Campions left the city to escape the summer heat, they traveled to their lodge at Twin Lakes, south of Leadville, built in 1895 and situated at the water's edge. Most rooms had fireplaces, including the game room. The lodge, almost 100 feet in length, featured a music room, a library, a smoking room, and bedrooms on the second level. It was furnished in typical rustic fashion, with wicker, comfortable rockers, and elk antlers over the mantels.

A power plant supplied electricity to the house and outbuildings. It was a gathering place for many of the family's friends and associates, and scores of guests partook of the Campions' hospitality over the years. Hunting, fishing, and horseback riding were just a few of the diversions found here.

Campion's death in 1916 set in motion a chain of events that gave the home the nickname "House of Sorrows." In 1917, his oldest son, John Jr., who had secretly married a year earlier while on break from Dartmouth College, lost his wife to illness. In 1921, Mrs. Campion's beloved brother died suddenly. In that same year, Roland Campion, her youngest son, was found dead in bed of a seizure while staying with

a schoolmate while on break from Philips Academy in New Hampshire. The shock broke her health, and she died less than a year later at the age of forty-eight, leaving her eldest son and two daughters, Helen and Phyllis, to survive her. Very soon afterward, Campion Sr.'s close associate in the Little Jonny Mine, J.J. Brown, died unexpectedly. Then Phyllis was stricken with a serious illness and was hospitalized. It was while she was bedridden that the only surviving son, John Jr., was killed in an auto accident in October 1923, at the age of twenty-seven, after having been on a duck-hunting trip near Leadville. He had become engaged only a few months earlier. Phyllis Campion was not told of her brother's death until after she was fully recovered. The following year, Dr. J.F. Nagle

The main hall of the Campion residence at Eighth Avenue and Logan Street.

Photo courtesy of John C. Mulvihill

motored from New York to Denver to announce his engagement to Helen Campion. Running late, he changed places with his chauffeur, stepped on the gas, and lost control of the car. He was pronounced dead at the scene.

Helen and Phyllis Campion were left with only each other. The house was put on the market, and the now very wealthy sisters set about traveling as an escape from their distress. But it was to shadow the family still. Helen soon met and married Harry Mulvihill, a Denver insurance broker. Their wedding was the social event of the 1927 season, and they decided to move back into the mansion on Logan Street together, the house that had been Helen's home since childhood.

A woman of many facets, Mrs. Mulvihill attended the University of Denver and Columbia University and held a bachelor of arts degree. During World War II, she prepared lectures and courses for the noncommissioned officer's school at Lowry Field and for general military training of Lowry Field personnel. She was also director of Pro Musica and the University Civic Theater of the University of Denver. She was a member of the National Council of Catholic Women, the Junior League, the University Club, and the Denver Press Club.

The Mulvihills had three sons, John C., Henry, and George. John remembers growing up in the Logan Street mansion: "We had a lot of fun, with the pool table and the bowling alley. Kid's stuff. We ran with the neighborhood gang. My brothers and I sold nightcrawlers at a stand we built on the corner, and also sold lemonade to people passing by our street. We used to go sledding down Logan Street in the winter, which shows how little traffic there was back then." By then, times had changed in the neighborhood. "When we were growing up," he added, "the top floor wasn't used as a ballroom anymore. A model train set ran completely around the top floor instead. Our dad used it as much as we did."

In 1940, the Mulvihills gave up the house on Logan Street and built a new home at 222 Gaylord Street in the country-club district for themselves and their three young sons. But all was not happy in the

Mulvihill household. The marriage was tumultuous, and the couple had separated briefly as early as 1931. In May 1942, Helen Mulvihill obtained a restraining order to keep her husband from entering their house, and she filed for a divorce. Harry Mulvihill packed two suitcases, left the house, and the next day was found slumped in the front seat of his car, fifty-four miles east of Denver, dead of an apparent accidental drug overdose.

Helen Campion Mulvihill married again the following year, to George Cook, a close friend of earlier days. She died at the age of forty-eight in November 1947.

When the Mulvihills gave up the Logan Street mansion in 1940, it passed into the hands of Clarence Daly, a successful insurance executive and nephew of Mrs. Campion. That same year, Claude K. Boettcher, son of Campion's business partner Charles Boettcher, offered to purchase the house for use by the Denver County Medical Society, an offer that was ultimately refused. Boettcher had proposed to make an outright gift of the property to the society. The rejection stemmed from the prohibitive costs of remodeling and building an auditorium in the house, plus installing of a fireproof library that would house the $150,000 collection of books owned by the society. It was also felt that the location was not suitable.

Boettcher eventually did purchase the property, and the house was turned over to the Denver chapter of the American Red Cross through a gift from the Boettcher Foundation. The new headquarters was opened to the public and to various volunteer activities of the Red Cross. The headquarters was formerly located in the Schuyler mansion at 300 East Eighth Avenue. That property continued to house Red Cross offices until it was torn down in the 1960s. One attraction for accepting the Campion house was that it was ready for immediate use without expenditure of funds. The original stables were converted to utilitarian use.

The house was used by the Red Cross until 1962, when the organization moved to new quarters in south Denver. For the next year, it sat vacant on its expansive grounds, derelict and forgotten, broken

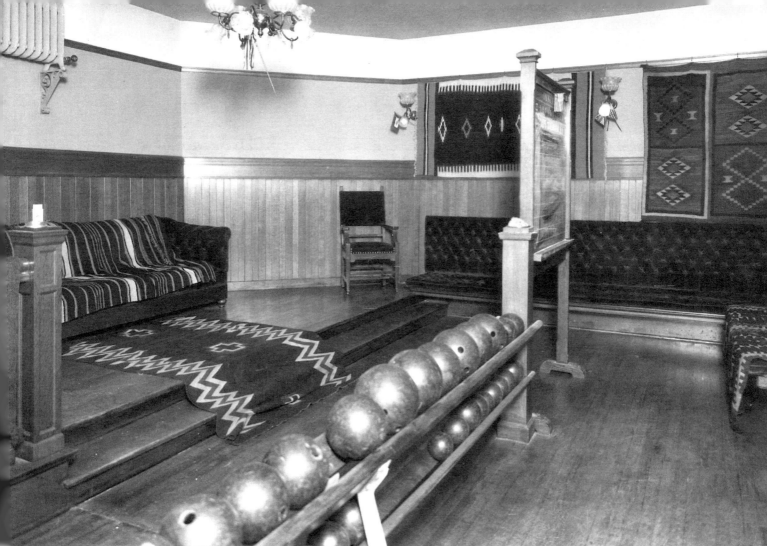

The basement bowling alley was a novelty for its time and was often the center of entertainment at the Campion house. Many tuxedoed men and jewel-bedecked women tried their hand after dinner.

glass littering its floors, walls and woodwork vandalized, and a yard filled with weeds and debris. A string of teenagers passed through the open house, taking fixtures and other souvenirs, and damaged the windows, the ornamental plaster, and the grand staircase. All that remained of its former glory were the large plaster medallions on the ceiling in the music room.

Two investors bought the property, and Lawrence Phipps III, scion of another important Denver family, took over a ninety-nine-year lease with plans to build a fifteen-story apartment building on the site. In late 1963, demolition began on the mansion, and one of Denver's most celebrated homes became nothing but a distant memory.

After the death of John Campion Sr., the lodge at Twin Lakes was sold and remodeled into the Hotel Campion. It burned to the ground in the mid-1920s.

John Campion Sr. was inducted into the National Mining Hall of Fame, located in Leadville, in September 2003, attended by numerous descendants.

John C. Mulvihill, who received his law degree at the University of Colorado at Boulder and is now semiretired, spent his first twelve years at 800 Logan Street. An avid outdoorsman, he enjoys fly fishing and is proud of the fact that he has climbed "almost" all of Colorado's Fourteeners.

Henry Mulvihill, also an outdoorsman and golfer, is a practicing attorney, having attained his degree at the University of Denver.

George Mulvihill, brother of John and Henry, died in 1990.

Chapter 9

CHARLES BOETTCHER HOUSE

1201 GRANT STREET

ARCHITECT: JOHN J. HUDDART

BUILT: 1890

One of the most recognized names in early Colorado history is that of Charles Boettcher, patriarch of an enterprising family that eventually controlled a vast international business empire. Born in 1852 in Colleda, Germany, Boettcher came to America at the age of seventeen and was caught up in the entrepreneurial spirit of the open West. He started his career as a merchant in Cheyenne, Wyoming, but before long he settled in Colorado, operating a hardware store out of Fort Collins. He opened more hardware and supply stores in Greeley and Boulder, then went on to Leadville, which was riding the wave of a huge silver boom. He began investing his earnings in mining and cattle ranching and was remarkably astute in his business decisions. He came to Denver a success. He began expanding his cattle and hardware businesses. He also founded the Western Packing Company, Denver's first, as an outlet for his cattle business. He later sold the Western Packing Company to Swift and Company at a large profit.

Boettcher was a pioneer in the Colorado sugar-beet industry, investing large sums of money in the cultivation and processing of sugar beets and entering into partnership with Chester S. Morey in founding the Great Western Sugar Company.

Another area of enterprise soon attracted his attention. Noticing that a great deal of cement used in local construction was being brought in from out of state, he founded the Colorado Cement

Author's Collection

Charles and Fannie Boettcher in the late 1870s.

and Denver National Bank and established the Boettcher Foundation, which operates today. He helped fund, along with his son, the construction of Boettcher School for special-needs children. Charles Boettcher, Sr. was, at one time or another, associated with many of Colorado's early business leaders, including Chester S. Morey, Dennis Sullivan, Julius Myers, Adolph Zang, and Horace Bennett.

Boettcher married Fannie Cowan in 1874, when he was working out of Fort Collins. She had moved there the previous year from Missouri, seeking a better climate for her poor health. A son, Claude Kedzie Boettcher, was born in 1875, followed by a daughter, Ruth, in 1890. They were soon ensconced in their new mansion at the northwest corner of Twelfth Avenue and Grant Street, along Denver's growing "Millionaire's Row," although Boettcher had yet to earn the title "Millionaire."

Boettcher's work occupied a great deal of his time, and Fannie filled her time with charitable work and

Company and later the Ideal Cement Company, with plants in Portland, Colorado, and outside of Fort Collins. He expanded his interest to railroads and utilities, including the installation of electric lights in Leadville and, later, Salt Lake City and St. Louis. He had investments in First National Bank

The Charles Boettcher residence at 1201 Grant Street, built in the middle of "Millionaire's Row."

Denver Public Library Western History Collection

world travel. Her donations to worthy causes were legion, and she was an important benefactress of the Children's Hospital and the Kent School for Girls. She was also a quiet and somewhat reclusive person, and not much was printed about her in the press. She did oversee her various investments and remained active in other business interests.

The Boettchers separated in 1920, and Charles Boettcher first went to live in the former home of his business partner, John Campion, at 800 Logan Street, adjacent to the home of his son, Claude Boettcher. He then found accommodations at the Denver Club and the Denver Athletic Club before taking up residence in the Brown Palace Hotel, of which he was a major owner. He died in 1948 at the age of ninety-six. Fannie remained by herself in the Grant Street mansion.

The Boettcher house was designed by J.J. Huddart and featured many historic furnishings, some dating back to colonial America. The house had the usual appointments of cut-glass and stained-glass windows, brass lighting fixtures, and generous rooms. While not as exuberantly decorated as those of the neighboring residences, the house exuded a quiet elegance that spoke of solid sensibilities. A variety of woodwork was found throughout the house. Fannie Boettcher was an astute collector of art and had acquired many interesting and expensive pieces on her travels throughout the world. Many of her purchases were Asian artifacts, including fire screens, stitched silk wall hangings, and handwoven rugs. One of the rooms was completely furnished with Japanese decorations, while another room was filled with pieces of Delft porcelain. The house was also filled with pieces from Germany, France, and Italy. Huddart also designed the nearby John Creswell house at 1244 Grant Street, which survives today.

Fannie Boettcher spent her last years cloistered in her Grant Street mansion, shutters closed and iron gate locked, and died in 1952 at the age of ninety-seven after spending the last year of her life at Rose Memorial Hospital. She was one of the very few at that time to retain original ownership of her Capitol Hill mansion. Most of her neighbors had long since died or abandoned the area.

The Boettcher house was torn down the following year to make way for the new Colorado Department of Employment Building, which uses the facility to this day. The huge Fullerton residence, just west facing Sherman Street, was wrecked at the same time. The fact that this stretch of Grant Street was once one of Denver's finest residential areas is lost today to the thousands of motorists and pedestrians who pass the present-day apartment buildings, hotels, offices, shops, and parking lots. Vestiges of the Gilded Age still show themselves occasionally: a base to an old hitching post, or old sandstone stairs leading to nothing but an asphalt parking lot. Every few blocks, an old dwelling survives intact as a monument to times long gone.

Chapter 10

Claude K. Boettcher House

400 East Eighth Avenue

Architects: Willis Marean
& Albert J. Norton

Built: 1907

I n 1901, Walter Scott Cheesman purchased sixteen lots at the southeast corner of Eighth Avenue and Logan Street, a location that was considered one of the finest building sites in Capitol Hill. He purchased the property with the intention of building his family a fine residence that would compliment a man of his stature. Cheesman, namesake of Cheesman Reservoir and Dam, Cheesman Park, and the Cheesman Memorial Pavilion, was closely identified with the building of early Denver and is considered among a group of pioneers of major importance. He began his career in the 1860s with a small drugstore at Fifteenth and Blake streets and from that built a fortune of a size then unparalleled in the region. He was a prominent player in early land speculation, buying up large parcels and selling them for top dollar as the region grew. He owned the land that the State Capitol Building was built upon, and he owned a large house adjacent to that site at 1540 Lincoln Street. He was a major owner of the monopolistic Denver Union Water Company, and he branched out into railroads and other successful ventures. For a time, Cheesman was one of the largest land owners in the city.

He never lived to see the completion of the Logan Street house, as he died suddenly in 1907. His widow, Alice, a leader of Denver's club, civic, and social life, decided to go ahead with plans to finish the monumental residence on the land her husband had bought. Under the direction of the noted architecture team of Marean and Norton, who at that time had offices in the McPhee Building downtown at

The Claude K. Boettcher residence, one of Denver's most widely known mansions, exudes a quiet colonial charm.

Seventeenth Street and Glenarm Place, construction commenced. The Cheesmans' daughter, Gladys, was married in the house in 1908, soon after its completion, to John Evans, scion of one of Denver's most well-known pioneer families. The twenty-seven-room, three-story house was built in a modified colonial style and was furnished in the solid but restrained style of the day.

Mrs. Cheesman lived there with a retinue of help until her death in 1923. Later that same year, the house was purchased by Claude K. Boettcher, financial and industrial giant and son of Charles and Fannie Boettcher.

Claude Boettcher was born in Boulder in 1875, when his father was running a successful hardware business there. As a debonair young man, he followed his father's footsteps into the business world, gaining considerable expertise. He was involved with a number of successful ventures: the Colorado Fuel and Iron Company, of which he became a director; the Brown Palace Hotel on Broadway and Seventeenth Street, owned by his father; the Great Western Sugar Company; other sugar-beet processors;

Ideal Cement, which was a company developed by his father, and to which Claude Boettcher succeeded as president on the death of his father in 1948; and he was a major investor in the Public Service Company. He also sat on the board of the New Markham Investment Company and the General Securities Company and was part owner of the Big Horn Cattle Company.

Boettcher's money also went into the Denver Dry Goods Company, the Denver and Intermountain Railway, and the Denver Tramway Corporation, which was a forerunner of Denver's present public-transportation system. As an avid and experienced pilot, he invested, with his son Charles Boettcher II, in the Aviation Corporation, and he was instrumental in promoting aviation throughout the area. When the Denver Municipal Airport was built, Boettcher helped to popularize air travel in Colorado. There seemed to be little in the state that Boettcher or his money didn't touch.

Boettcher made large financial gifts to many charitable causes, and through the Boettcher Foundation, formed in 1937, his and his father's philanthropies became a major benefit to such institutions as the Denver Zoo, the Denver Museum of Natural History (both in City Park), Children's Hospital, the Community Chest (later to become United Way), and the Boettcher School (adjacent to Children's Hospital), a facility for special-needs children.

In 1947, Claude Boettcher was listed as one of the sixty-four men who ran America, according to author John Gunther in the *Magazine of the Year*. He was also named one of the best-dressed men in America by a team of Fifth Avenue tailors. He was a graduate of Harvard University with an engineering degree and was married in 1900 to De Allen McMurtry, whose father, John, owned a sprawling Italian Renaissance masterpiece at 700 Washington Street, now the site of a high-rise apartment building. The couple had one son, Charles Boettcher II. Claude Boettcher divorced and married again in 1920, to Edna Case McElveen.

When Boettcher took possession of the Logan Street mansion, moderate structural changes were made to the interior. However, the restrained ambiance of the Cheesmans was replaced with a staggering extravagance in furnishings. The front entrance of the mansion opens into a vast hallway running the length of the house to the Palm Room. This opens to a large, sloping garden featuring fountains and stone steps leading to a variety of trees, shrubs, and flowers.

The large drawing room off the main hall boasts a large crystal chandelier that once hung in the White House and dates from 1800. Two wall-sized Goeblin tapestries were bought from the Russian government for $50,000 and ensconced in this room, along with priceless paintings, bronzes, and carved jade and quartz pieces. The library is adjacent to this room, and the prized piece here is a large desk made for Louis IV. The main floor also contains the dining

The garden to the east of the Claude Boettcher mansion.
Author's Collection

room, with walls of solid walnut, stained pale green. The dining table is ornately carved, with sitting lions bearing the weight of the tabletop. The chairs are also heavily carved and upholstered in rich tapestry. Service rooms are also located on this floor.

The Palm Room was famous in its day for its unique style and breathtaking beauty. Originally a small sunporch, it was enlarged twice, the last time to its current size of sixty by seventy feet. When the Boettchers owned the house, this room was furnished entirely in white, against a backdrop of palm trees and other greenery. Just inside the entrance is a large fountain. The room is lighted by an immense crystal chandelier. The floor is white marble, and the white columns around the room give an impression of a Grecian villa. The room was walled in with glass and offers a view of the gardens.

Claude Boettcher died in 1957, and after the death of his widow the following year, the house became the property of the Boettcher Foundation, which, in turn, offered the mansion to the state of Colorado. Ideas for an executive mansion had been bandied about for decades, but nothing had ever come of it. The fact that the Boettcher property was desirable, not only for its location, but its size, was too appealing to resist. There were major obstacles to overcome, however. For one, not everybody was keen on the idea of a governor's mansion. Then-governor Steve McNichols, an early supporter of the plan, was living with his family in a comfortable home in the Crestmoor neighborhood, and many voiced their opinion that the governor ought to live like everyone else. Others thought the mansion too extravagant and that the money ought to be spent on other, more practical needs.

In early 1959, the Colorado legislature turned down the offer. The Boettcher Foundation then announced its plans to auction the furniture, demolish the mansion, and sell the lots for development, as no other feasible use for it could be found. By this time, however, the mansion had its boosters, and the idea was kept alive. Apparently, the threat of losing one of Capitol Hill's most well-known icons became all too real, and later that year, the state accepted the gift. Remodeling and renovation were necessary,

and structural work included replastering, rewiring, and replacing much of the outdated plumbing. The second floor was made into family living quarters by the addition of two bathrooms to the existing two, and by turning the second-floor landing into a family room. The first floor has changed little over the

years, with minor exceptions, from the days when the Boettchers entertained their friends and business associates.

Public tours of the main-floor rooms are given free of charge. For more information, contact the Colorado Historical Society.

The Palm Room, the scene of some of Denver's most celebrated parties.

Denver Public Library Western History Collection

Chapter II

Charles Boettcher II House

777 Washington Street

Architect: Harry Manning

Built: circa 1920

Charles Boettcher II, the son of Claude K. Boettcher, and the grandson of Charles Boettcher Sr., was born in Denver in September 1901. He attended Yale University and, after graduation, became a director of some of the varied Boettcher enterprises. He became interested in flying at an early age, and after getting his pilot's license, he purchased his own plane. In the mid-1920s, he flew mail between Denver and Pueblo. He persuaded his father and grandfather to purchase land in northeast Denver for use as headquarters for the 120th Observation Squadron. He was a commanding officer in the Civil Air Patrol. He also served as a director of Western Airlines and was instrumental in bringing United Airlines to Denver.

Charles Boettcher II was a partner with his father in many of the vast Boettcher concerns, and he sat on the board of the Boettcher Foundation. He was also on the board of Boettcher & Company and Ideal Cement Company, and he held positions at Boettcher Realty Company, the Potash Company of America, and the American Crystal Sugar Company. He was a director of the Community Chest and was a trustee of the Denver Art Museum and the Denver Zoo. Boettcher was also a member of the Civic Progress Commission and was a director of Denver National Bank from 1928 to 1935. Taking up his family's civic responsibility, he gave generously and quietly to many deserving charities.

One of the more whimsical houses on Capitol Hill, but one with a dark history, was that of Charles Boettcher II.

This house was deceptively charming, for it was the scene of more than one misfortune. On February 12, 1933, Charles Boettcher II was kidnapped from his garage at gunpoint in the presence of his wife, Anna Lou, just before midnight. She was given a ransom note demanding $60,000 for his safe return. Boettcher was held for half a month on a South Dakota farm while his kidnappers negotiated the ransom payment. It was soon paid by the family, and he was released in a field about twelve miles northeast of Denver. Following leads, local police captured Verne Sankey in the Chicago area a few months after the kidnapping. Sankey fingered Gordon Alcorn as an accomplice. Two others were also implicated for their lesser roles in the crime and were soon arrested. While waiting for his arraignment, Sankey, vowing not to "take the rap," committed suicide in his cell in a South Dakota jailhouse, using neckties tied together and strung over his bunk. Alcorn, along with the two others involved in the plot, Carl Pearce

and Arthur Youngberg, pleaded guilty, and all three were sentenced to long prison terms.

In 1941, Anna Lou Boettcher, despondent over prolonged health problems, committed suicide in the house by shooting herself in the head. Boettcher remarried a few years later, this time to Mae Scott Foster, and they divided their time traveling between their homes in San Francisco, and Hawaii, and their suite at the Brown Palace Hotel. Boettcher died in 1963 after years of ill health, leaving two daughters by his first wife but no sons to carry on the Boettcher name.

The Washington Street house was sold in the early 1950s, and for a time it was operated as a small hotel. In August 1956, the mansion was raided by police, who uncovered an elaborate gambling operation in the basement. Illegal crap games and other games of chance were discovered, along with stacks of poker

chips and pairs of dice. Eight people were arrested on vice charges. The mansion was closed up and sat empty and derelict in a weed-choked lot.

Police were called to the property on many occasions to check on reports of vandalism and break-ins.

Much of the interior was destroyed or damaged, and the city stepped in and declared the house a public nuisance. It was wrecked in 1963 to make way for a high-rise apartment building. The destruction of this house, more than practically any other in the area, symbolized the beginning of the end of an era.

The drawing room of the Charles Boettcher II residence.

Denver Public Library Western History Collection

Chapter 12

JAMES McCLURG/ TEMPLE BUELL HOUSE

906 GRANT STREET

ARCHITECT: UNKNOWN

BUILT: 1900

Two of the most prominent houses along Grant Street, the McClurg/ Buell house and the J.S. Brown house, were built across the street from each other. James McClurg built a yellow twenty-six-room house for himself and his bride, the former Marcia Moffat, daughter of the railroad tycoon, at 906 Grant Street, in 1900. The couple had previously lived at 1089 East Colfax when that avenue was considered an elite thoroughfare. When McClurg died in 1909, his widow spent more of her time traveling, and she died in Paris in 1929. The mansion was sold in 1910 to Otto Sauer, who had previously lived at 1517 Logan Street. Sauer started his career as a merchant in Central City during the Gold Rush days and became so successful that he was able to expand his business into what was then one of the largest mercantile operations in the region. He was a founder, and later president, of the First National Bank of Central City, and he moved his family to Denver in the early 1890s. Along with James B. Grant, Joseph Thatcher, and others, he was a founder and director of the Denver National Bank and was one of the founders of the region's first cement plant.

Temple Hoyne Buell purchased the house after Sauer's death in the early 1920s. Buell was a well-known architect, real-estate developer, and entrepreneur, namesake of the Buell Theater in the Denver Center complex, Buell & Company, and the Temple Buell Foundation. Buell had married Marjorie McIntosh, heiress to the Household Finance Corporation. He was responsible for the design

Built for James McClurg and his wife, this house later became the home of prominent Denver architect Temple Buell.

and/or construction of some of the state's most distinguished buildings, including Lincoln, Kennedy, Regis, and Mann schools; some of the buildings on the campus of the University of Colorado in Boulder; the New Customs House downtown; and the Paramount Theater—Denver's art-deco showcase. The Buell firm also erected the Lincoln Park housing project in 1940 at Colfax, just south of the present Auraria campus. Lincoln Park has since been demolished. Temple Buell was part of the large team of architects that designed Denver's City & County Building, opened in 1932.

In the 1920s, Buell had bought a large parcel of land located at First Avenue and University Boulevard. It was nothing but a muddy, weed-filled area. His family and associates thought he had thrown his money away on foolish speculation. The city leased part of the property for use as a garbage dump. That was all to change, however. By the early 1950s, the area was built up sufficiently that Buell's land was ripe for development. Soon, construction began on the Cherry Creek Shopping Center, Denver's premiere shopping area. It was immediately successful and

made Temple Buell even wealthier than he had been. He devoted his later years to charities and civic work, donating large amounts of money to the University of Colorado School of Medicine, the Columbia School of Architecture, and the Colorado Women's College.

Buell sold the Grant Street house in the late 1930s and moved closer to Cherry Creek. He was divorced in 1958. He died in 1990 at the age of ninety-six and is interred in the family mausoleum that he designed himself at Fairmont Cemetery. At the time Buell gave up the Grant Street mansion, the neighborhood had changed radically. Most of the families that lived along this street had long since departed, and the surviving houses were being used as schools, or rooming houses, or they were boarded shut. The Buell house was operated as a rooming house for thirty to thirty-five paying guests. In its last few years, it sat empty and derelict in a weed-filled lot waiting for the wrecking ball. It was demolished in the late 1960s to make way for the new high-rise Financial Programs Companies Building, a national mutual-funds company.

Chapter 13

John Sidney Brown House

909 Grant Street

Architects: Aaron Gove & Thomas Walsh

Built: 1891

John Sidney Brown and his brother, Junius, were instrumental in the early development of the city of Denver. Together they formed and operated the highly successful Brown Mercantile Company, providing wholesale merchandise to many of the traders and store owners around the state. John Brown had been living in a fine home downtown at the northeast corner of Fourteenth and Stout streets, which later became the site of the popular Auditorium Hotel (now a parking lot). He decided that he would follow his peers, many of whom had already built their mansions along the streets of Capitol Hill, and constructed his massive, five-story, twenty-three-room monument to capitalism in the area of Capitol Hill known as "Quality Hill." The home became known locally as "John Brown's Schoolhouse," so named for his ten children, five with his first wife and five with his second.

John Sidney Brown was born in Conneaut, Ohio, in 1833, where he was educated. He joined his brother Junius in 1858 in Atchison, Kansas, where they became involved in the lumber business. The Brown brothers came to Colorado around 1860 and immediately became involved in the freighting and lumber businesses. John Brown's first foray into the mercantile business came as a result of his partnership with A.B. Daniels. Together they opened a grocery business at Fifteenth and Blake streets, but they lost everything in a fire in 1863. The business was rebuilt, and Daniels retired from the company in 1868. At that time, John and his brother Junius founded

J.S. Brown & Brother. Their success was rapid. In 1893, the name was changed to the J.S. Brown Mercantile Company. John Brown also had interests in the Colorado Milling and Elevator Company, along with real-estate holdings and railroads. He was also an investor in the Denver Tramway Company, the forerunner of our present bus system.

Brown's Grant Street palace was frequented by many illustrious visitors, not the least of which was William "Buffalo Bill" Cody, who spent many hours sitting on the front porch telling stories of the Old West to the Brown children. Inside, the rooms were spacious, connected by wide hallways finished in various hardwoods. The dining room could seat forty guests comfortably, and the library walls were of sycamore and embossed leather. Ornate fireplaces were in most rooms. Most of the upstairs bedrooms were in bird's-eye maple. A billiards room was in the basement, and a ballroom, very much a standard feature at the turn of the century, covered most of the top floor. The plumbing throughout the house was copper. The lighting fixtures, doorknobs, and hinges were solid brass.

John Brown died in 1913, and the house was sold three years later to William Blayney, of the Blayney-Murphy Meat Packing Company (later bought by the Cudahy Company). William Blayney was an officer with the Hallack Investment Company, which was owned by his wife's family, and he was a director of the First National Bank. He also served as treasurer for the Moffat Tunnel Commission and was involved with David Moffat and Walter S. Cheesman in the Denver Union Water Company in the days when Denver's water supply was still privately operated. He was also president of the Market Company and a vice-president of the Denver Packing and Provision Company.

Blayney died in 1936. The house was sold to Mrs. Verner Z. Reed, an active social and civic leader and widow of the highly successful mining engineer. Mrs. Reed donated the property to the University of Denver, and for years it was run by the Lamont School of Music, directed by Florence Lamont Hinman. Hinman had previously operated a school out of the old William Berger mansion at 1170 Sherman

Street (since demolished). She ran the school until 1953, when she left, but she continued to teach and lecture until her death in 1969. The Lamont School soon moved out and continues to this day close to the University of Denver campus.

The house now sat empty for the first time, too large to be used as a residence and too ungainly to be used for much else. The J.S. Brown mansion was torn down in June 1968. The property has been used since as a parking lot for the Financial Programs Companies, located across Grant Street at 906, the site of the former James McClurg/Temple Buell mansion. The J.S. Brown Mercantile Building, at 1634 Eighteenth Street, is now the Wynkoop Brewing Company.

Junius Brown, the brother of John Sidney Brown and partner in the Brown Mercantile Company, had ensconced his family in the former Henry Wise Hobson mansion at 933 Pennsylvania Street. Hobson was an attorney specializing in mining law and handled many of the early cases from Colorado's most colorful mining period. He was also president of the International Trust Company.

The gray stone mansion was built around 1897 and sold to Brown in 1903. Brown and his wife were civic leaders who previously lived downtown at Fourteenth and Welton streets, in a large house that was later turned into apartments and subsequently torn down in the 1920s. Junius Brown was a founder of the Denver Gas and Electric Company and the Denver Tramway Corporation. He also invested in railroads.

An avid art collector, he constructed a special gallery on the north side of the Pennsylvania Street house to display his many paintings and pieces of sculpture. The house was a center of activity among his peers and business associates, and when he died in 1908, his widow continued holding court there until her death in 1937.

The house was sold again, this time to Mr. and Mrs. Frank Freyer. The Freyers were also art collectors, and many of their pieces are now in the Denver Art Museum. Mr. Freyer died in 1947, and his wife lived

The elaborate woodwork and plaster decoration of the John Sidney Brown dining room.

on in the mansion until she died in 1970. The house sat empty until it was reduced to rubble in 1972 to make way for a series of townhouses.

In November 1947, an unidentified man was found slumped across the bed in a second-floor room at the old Adams Hotel at Eighteenth and Welton streets. There was a bullet hole in his head. Three days later, it was revealed that the man was John Sidney Brown, Jr., son of the builder of 909 Grant. He had become company president upon the senior's death and had acquired a taste for lavish spending and powerful, expensive automobiles. He had attended the best schools, was a member of all the exclusive clubs, and ran in the tightest social circles. But the business was a victim of the Great Depression, like so many others, and he was forced to sell to the Morey Mercantile Company, his only close competitor. He retired, and in the next two decades, the vast amounts of money formerly at his disposal had dwindled considerably. He checked into the hotel under an assumed name. The body was found clutching a note to his wife. With one bullet, he closed an important chapter of Denver history.

Chapter 14

CHARLES HUGHES HOUSE

1200 GRANT STREET

ARCHITECT: HENRY T.E. WENDELL

BUILT: CIRCA 1900

U p the street from the J.S. Brown and Temple Buell houses was the Charles Hughes residence, at 1200 Grant Street. This house, built about 1900, was constructed of brown sandstone at a cost of $40,000. Hughes, a prominent attorney, was born in Kingston, Missouri, in 1853. He received his law degree from the University of Missouri and attended the University of Denver. After graduation, he taught public school and later taught college classes. He became a professor of mining law at the University of Denver and lectured at the Harvard Law School. He established his law practice in Denver in 1887 and was soon sought out for his knowledge on complicated business and industrial laws.

Hughes's brilliant legal tactics and forceful charisma soon attracted the attention of prominent city leaders, and he became counsel to many of the most powerful of Denver's politicians and capitalists. He became associated with Western Union, the Union Pacific Railroad, and the Denver & Rio Grande Railroad. He was also a co-owner of the *Denver Post*, before that struggling newspaper was sold to Harry H. Tammen and Frederick G. Bonfils. The latter turned the *Post* into one of the state's most successful ventures. Politically involved, Hughes was the unanimous choice of the Democratic Convention in 1908 for U.S. senator, to succeed Henry M. Teller. His outspoken political views naturally clashed with those of his neighbors and helped to create a long-running feud with his next-door neighbor, George Baxter. The *Denver Times* reported on this test of wills and influence:

The Charles Hughes house sat across Grant Street from that of Charles Boettcher. After the house's demolition, the site was used for years as a parking lot.

It appears that we may never hear the last of the Baxters. The latest sensation is that the Baxter house, instead of having been bought by Tyson Dines for himself, was bought by him for Gerald Hughes. Wherefore, it of course appears that the Hughes family were willing to pay to get the Baxters out of the neighborhood. The Hughes pride is a proverb, and the Baxter stick-to-itiveness is another. The two qualities did not make an agreeable combination. When the bombshell fell into the Hughes family announcing Cornelia Baxter's engagement, they consoled themselves with the thought that of course the Baxters would leave the house next door. It now appears that when the Baxters came back and showed no disposition to move the Hughes family took steps to make them do it by offering, through an agent, such a good price for the house that the Baxters could not afford to refuse it. If Baxter had known, however, that he was selling his house to Hughes, the deal would never have been closed. The house has been advertised for sale. It is hardly likely that Hughes would care to live there.

[The Baxter house, at 1212 Grant Street, was later sold to oilman Frank Kistler and was torn down about the same time as the Charles Hughes house.]

In 1909, Hughes was elected to the U.S. Senate on the Democratic ticket and served until his death in 1911. He was also a member of the American Bar Association and the American Institute of Mining Engineers.

Hughes was survived by three sons, Gerald, Lafayette, and Berrien, and a daughter, Mrs. W. Woodruff, Jr. Gerald Hughes, a successful financier, attorney, and socialite, became a Colorado senator from 1902 to 1908 and was instrumental in the planning of the Moffat Tunnel. He died in 1957.

Lafayette Hughes was involved in his father's business ventures and expanded some of the family's holdings. When Charles Hughes died, his widow continued to live in the Grant Street house. It later became the home of Berrien Hughes, sportsman and socialite, until his death in a skiing accident in 1939.

The Hughes family retained ownership of the mansion but had homes of their own. Lafayette Hughes built a sprawling, thirty-six-room, Mediterranean-style mansion at 41 Polo Club Circle, on property owned by the Hughes family and bounded by South University Boulevard, South Steele Street, East Alameda Avenue, and East Exposition Avenue. This land had been developed earlier for use as a polo playing field. The three-story residence, designed by Fisher & Fisher about 1926, was modeled around large, open hallways, with spacious rooms. The ceilings of many of these rooms were the focal point, with painted frescoes and elaborate plasterwork. The main floor consisted of a large drawing room, a dining room, a wood-paneled library, a breakfast room, a kitchen, and a conservatory. A long central hall, with massive pillars and a decorated wooden ceiling, ran almost the length of the house. The drawing room was in its own wing and featured a raised platform where musicals and other entertainment were performed. Originally, the house was furnished in a Venetian style, with large, ornate mirrors and Italian-style tables and chairs, but later it was refurnished in a more informal style. Lafayette Hughes maintained this house until his death in 1958, when it was sold to Mrs. McIntosh Buell, former wife of Temple Hoyne Buell. The house was featured on a number of Denver house tours before it was wrecked in the 1970s and the land was sold for the development of exclusive residential properties.

One of Denver's largest, yet least publicized, mansions was well hidden from public view. Gerald Hughes built his gigantic, forty-two-room manor house overlooking the grounds of the Denver Country Club, adjacent to the equally large John Morey

The exterior of the Lafayette Hughes residence on the polo grounds.

Colorado State Historical Society

One of the largest of all the city's mansions, the Gerald Hughes residence sat hidden away from view, overlooking the Denver Country Club.

mansion. The 23,000-square-foot house, at 1919 East Alameda Avenue, was built of reinforced concrete with a stucco finish. It was designed by Fisher & Fisher in a modified Mediterranean style, with austere angles, tall, arched windows, and a red-tile roof. Originally furnished in an Italian and Spanish style, the rambling mansion contained carved and painted woodwork, antique Spanish doorways, custom-made chandeliers, and glazed tile flooring.

The living room contained a ceiling painted by the late Vance Kirkland, celebrated Denver artist and former head of the art department at the University of Denver. The fireplace was of marble. The dining-room ceiling was of molded plaster made specially by a firm in New York. The library, heavily paneled in walnut, held a large collection of books and artwork gathered from around the world. Much of the furniture was of museum quality and was collected during the Hughes's trips abroad.

The six acres of grounds were kept manicured by a retinue of gardeners and had winding walkways, numerous fountains, and a reflecting pool. Mrs. Hughes, a benefactress and founder of Children's Hospital, collected silver and china, and she kept a key with her at all times to unlock the vault where her treasures were stored. After Gerald Hughes's death, the house was put on the market. It was temporarily taken over by the American Institute of Interior Designers and was featured on a successful historic Denver house tour. The mansion was torn down in 1972 to make way for construction of seventeen luxury homesites.

The Grant Street mansion was sold by the family in 1958 and was demolished shortly thereafter. The property sat vacant for many years, sometimes being used for parking. In 1992, the Colorado Association of School Boards built their modern office building on the site.

Chapter 15

KARL SCHUYLER HOUSE

300 East Eighth Avenue
Architect: J.J. (Jacques) Benedict
Built: circa 1920

This home was first the residence of D.B. Turner. It later became the home of Senator Karl Cortlandt Schuyler (1877–1933), a descendant of General Philip Schuyler, who was a member of the Continental Congress. Senator Schuyler had made a considerable fortune investing in oil, mining, and real estate, and he served as Colorado senator from 1932 to 1933. He was instrumental in the formation of the Midwest Oil & Refining Company and was a director of the Denver National Bank. He was also one of the founders of the Community Chest of Denver, a member of the Colorado Bar Association, and a member of the board of trustees of the University of Denver.

When this house was built in the early part of the twentieth century, it featured leaded-glass windows, hand-painted tiles, a staircase with a handmade wrought-iron banister, and spacious rooms decorated in the Spanish style, popular in the 1920s. The floor plan was simple, with a large, central hall, a living room, and a dining room on the main level. Bedrooms and a sitting room were on the second floor, while rooms for the small staff were located in the basement.

The beautiful gardens to the south of the house were plotted around a sweeping double staircase that sloped from the back of the house gently down to the lawn, with columns on both sides and topped with an enclosed second-story balcony. The centerpiece of that stairway was a ram's-head fountain and pool.

A private residence for a relatively short time, the Karl Schuyler house was, for years, used by the Denver Chapter of the American Red Cross.

After Senator Schuyler's death, the house was rented out as a private residence. In 1939, the house was purchased from his widow, and plans were made to convert it into permanent headquarters for the Denver Chapter of the American Red Cross. They had been an agency of the Community Chest and were planning to move out of their quarters in the former L'Imperiale Hotel at 314 Fourteenth Street, in downtown Denver. This was met with serious protest from a group of neighbors, who feared that the introduction of the organization constituted a commercial enterprise in what was still a heavily, and wealthy, residential area.

At one zoning meeting, officials of the Red Cross explained that they intended to establish a bandage-making station, hold classes on sewing, and carry on its usual charitable work. It was also pointed out

that the former Moffat mansion, just across Eighth Avenue, was now being operated as a Greek fraternal organization. The zoning board deferred action for a number of weeks until it was decided that the Red Cross posed no threat to the neighborhood, and the plan moved forward. The house was used in that capacity for many years. In late 1963, plans were made to merge six chapters into a new headquarters being built in south Denver. After the Red Cross moved out, the house sat derelict in a weed-filled yard.

Windows and doors were boarded shut and shingles hung from its roof. The house was demolished in the mid-1960s, around the time when many Capitol Hill mansions were falling at a rapid rate. An office building was constructed in its place, and the address was changed to 780 Grant Street. It became offices for the Pitney-Bowes Company and is now used by the Denver Public Schools, Department of Technology Services.

The graceful double staircase to the south of the Schuyler house spoke of an era long forgotten.

Denver Public Library Western History Collection

Chapter 16

James B. Grant/A.E. Humphreys House

770 Pennsylvania Street

Architects: Theodore Boal & Frederick Harnois

Built: 1902

This house sat on property that took up a good portion of the block. It was originally built for James Benton Grant and was designed by Theodore Boal and F.I. Harnois, whose offices were located at 100 East Sixteenth Avenue. Grant had a long career connected with mining and smelting at the time when mining was one of the major industries of the state. He was born in Russell County, Alabama, in 1848. His father was a physician and cotton planter. James B. Grant attended Iowa Agricultural College. He went from there to Cornell University, then on to Freiburg, Germany, where he studied mineralogy.

When he came to Colorado in 1877, he became engaged in mining in the Central City area, then moved to Leadville when it was starting its famous boom. Grant erected one of the first major smelters in Leadville, and this laid the foundation to his fortune. He later came to Denver and organized the Omaha and Grant Smelter in north Denver. He was its vice-president from 1882 to 1899. The company was sold to the Guggenheim brothers, and Grant became chairman of the board of the American Smelting and Refining Company. He was also managing director of that company in Colorado.

Grant was also an organizer and director of the Denver National Bank and became involved in local politics. He was the first Democratic governor of the state (1883 to 1885) and a leader in Colorado business and political affairs.

The stately James B. Grant residence sits prominently atop a steep hill.

Grant married Mary Goodell in Leadville in 1881. They had two sons, Lester and James B., Jr.

At the turn of the century, the Grants were living in a large, shingle-style house at 1280 Grant Street, on the avenue that had become so desirable an address to Denver's prominent citizens. That house was torn down in the 1920s to make way for a row of storefronts. Those have since been demolished for a new row of small shops. The Grants lived at the Grant Street address until 1902, when construction was finished on what was arguably Denver's finest residence, a Colonial Revival mansion atop a hill at 770 Pennsylvania Street. It boasted thirty spacious rooms, high ceilings, and wide porches and balconies. The house was approached by a sweeping drive and by a shorter driveway that led to a multicar garage. Originally, a long stairway and walkway led to the front door from the street. It has since been removed.

James B. Grant died in November 1911 at Excelsior Springs, Missouri. Mrs. Grant sold the mansion in 1918 to the Humphreys family and moved to 100 South Franklin Street in the Country Club area, where she remained until her death in 1941.

Colonel Albert E. Humphreys was a multi-millionaire with interests ranging from oil and railroads to mining and real estate. He received his title of "colonel" as a young man serving on the governor's guard in his home state of West Virginia. Humphreys was at one time rated among the five richest men in Colorado. Born in 1860, he was educated locally and married Alice Boyd in 1887. The couple moved to Colorado a decade later. His first big success was the development of the Mesaba Iron Range, west of Duluth, Minnesota. That was followed by the Big Muddy Oil Field of Wyoming, another large discovery in Texas, and the famous Mexia, Texas, field, from which he realized a large portion of his wealth. He was a director of the Denver National Bank and also had oil holdings in Oklahoma during the boom of the late 1910s. Other investments included coal and lumber.

In May 1927, tragedy struck the house to the core. After getting up from the dinner table, Colonel Humphreys left his wife and guests to retire to his room. A short while later, a dinner guest went looking for Mr. Humphreys. He was found slumped against the wall with the lower half of his face destroyed from a buckshot blast. No shot was heard. He was conscious and bleeding, and when he realized he could not articulate, he motioned for a pen and paper. Humphreys wrote: "Give me chloroform and let me die." He was able to walk aided to the ambulance, which rushed him to Mercy Hospital, where doctors frantically tried to keep him alive. The attempts were unsuccessful, and Humphreys died shortly after surgery. His wife and two sons were with him when he died. He had been preparing to go on a hunting trip to his lodge at Wagon Wheel Gap. The trip was meant to be part of his recuperation from a bout of pneumonia. There was speculation that he had been cleaning his gun when it went off accidentally. That scenario was unlikely, however, as he had been around guns all of his life. A rumor surfaced, also, that Humphreys had been involved in dubious business dealings and that they were coming to light. Supposedly he had taken his own life in order to avoid testifying against his partners.

After his death, the Pennsylvania Street house went to his widow, Alice, and she continued to live there with her son, Ira, and his wife. In 1937, a rapid series of catastrophes were visited upon the Humphreys family. In one week's period, Ira Humphreys lost his stables at his Colorado ranch to a fire; his son, A. Putnam Humphreys, suffered fire damage at his Denver home; and Mrs. A. Putnam Humphreys suffered a fractured skull and had to be hospitalized as a result of an automobile accident. While she was recuperating, her house was robbed of more than $50,000 worth of jewelry and furs. This chain of events culminated with the sudden death of Alice Humphreys.

Ira Humphreys, an entrepreneur in his own right, was born in Charleston, West Virginia, in 1890. Humphreys attended the University of Colorado but dropped out when he married a childhood sweetheart, Lucille Pattison, in 1909. The senior

Drawing room of 770 Pennsylvania in the mid-1920s.

Colorado State Historical Society

Terra-cotta detailing of the Grant/Humphreys mansion.

also was an avid horseman. With Lafayette Hughes and others, he purchased land at University Boulevard and Alameda Avenue and founded the Denver Polo Club, immensely popular with Denver's "smart set." The playing field was sold off for exclusive homesites years ago.

Humphreys's first wife was a co-founder of the Junior League of Denver. She died in 1961. He remarried in 1962 to Mrs. Lu-Gray Dodge Brown. She died in 1972, and he followed her to the grave in 1976. He willed the house and grounds to the Colorado State Historical Society, and much of the

Humphreys at that time lived in a large house at 1019 Logan Street, the former home of William Mygatt, and the family moved together to the Pennsylvania Street mansion.

Humphreys was active in mining and real estate and was well known for his inventions, many of which were a boon to the mining industry. Ira Humphreys was a business partner with his brother, Albert E. Humphreys, Jr., and was president of the Curtiss-Humphreys Airplane Company and the Humphreys Engineering Company. He also was head of the Humphreys Gold Corporation. An avid pilot, he learned to fly at an early age and opened an airfield at East Twenty-Sixth Avenue and Olive Street. He was intensely interested in automobiles and was a member of the Denver Motor Club, a group of capitalists who were auto enthusiasts. He original furnishings were removed from the house and placed in storage. During this time, thieves broke in and made off with more than seventy-five items that included furniture, paintings, silver, and books valued in the thousands of dollars. What was not stolen was auctioned to the public in a sale that included the Chippendale dining set, consisting of a table, sixteen chairs, and two sideboards. A number of valuable Persian carpets were sold as well. The stolen items were recovered three months later in a moving van that had broken down at I-70 and Quebec Street and a suspect was arrested.

The Colorado State Historical Society operates the site to this day. The mansion is a popular destination for weddings, corporate meetings, bar and bat mitzvahs, memorial services, and birthday parties. The furnishings remain sympathetic to the period. The former four-car garage has been converted to offices for the Colorado Council on the Arts.

100 South Franklin Street, the home of Mrs. James B. Grant, from 1918 until her death in 1941.
Author's Collection

Chapter 17

ALBERT E. HUMPHREYS, JR. HOUSE

1022 HUMBOLDT STREET

ARCHITECTS: WILLIS MAREAN
        & ALBERT J. NORTON

BUILT: 1907

When Edward Stoiber made his millions mining the hills above Denver, he decided it was time that he and his wife, Lena, build a fine house worthy of a man of his stature. He liked the area around Cheesman Park and hired the architectural team Marean and Norton to design the massive structure. The partners were also responsible for a number of other well-known buildings, including the Denver Orphan's Home, the Greek Theater at Civic Center, the downtown YMCA Building, the Cheesman/Boettcher mansion, and the Cheesman Pavilion at Cheesman Park. But while plans were being considered for the house, Edward Stoiber was suddenly taken ill and died. Lena decided to go ahead with the plans, and work on the house commenced. When it was finished, it was one of the largest private homes in the area, at just over 16,000 square feet, with nine bedrooms and nine baths. Built for the purpose of becoming a social and entertainment center for the well-heeled of the city, the rooms were designed on a massive scale. The main-floor drawing room is more than forty feet in length, and the grand entrance hall is fifty feet long with an open balcony circling the second floor. The interior was, at one time, finished from top to bottom in white enamel—very costly when the house was built. The dining room can seat fifty comfortably. In the basement is a large swimming pool with beautifully tiled walls and a vaulted ceiling. A private elevator runs to the bedrooms on the second level. Also located in the basement is a regulation-size bowling alley, along with what was once a private barber salon. The heating plant for the house was located separately

A high wall hides the gargantuan dimensions of the Albert E. Humphreys, Jr. house at Tenth Avenue and Humboldt Street.

in the garage at the rear of the property and was accessible through a tunnel.

No expense was spared in the decoration of the mansion. The drapes were hung to Mrs. Stoiber's specifications by a famous Parisian firm. Italian painters and sculptors created the fireplace mantels and painted large murals. The house was filled with antique treasures purchased by both the Stoibers on their frequent trips to Europe. In order to protect these valuable artifacts, Lena Stoiber had solid-steel shutters installed at a cost of $4,500.

Lena married again, this time to Hugh Rood, a millionaire lumberman from Seattle. The couples' happiness was cut short, however, when he was lost in the *Titanic* disaster of 1912. Lena abandoned the house and escaped to Europe, where she stayed after deciding to put the house up for sale. She found a quick buyer in Verner Z. Reed, oilman, banker, mining man, and owner of one of the greatest art collections in the West—worth at that time well over $1 million. The Reeds had just returned from living abroad.

The Reeds entertained lavishly, and the house was a center of social activity. They lived in the house until Verner Reed's death, and his widow decided to sell and build her own mansion on Circle Drive in the late 1920s.

Albert E. Humphreys, Jr. and his wife, the former Ruth Boettcher, purchased the house and raised their two daughters, Charline and Ruth Augusta, there.

Not only was Humphreys involved in many of his father's business ventures, he was successful in his own right, having investments in oil, cattle, mining, and real estate. He was also associated with the Ideal Cement Company, founded and owned by his father-in-law, Charles Boettcher, Sr. Humphreys and his brother, Ira, owned several companies identified with mining, including the Humphreys Gold Cor-

Entrance hall of 1022 Humboldt Street in the mid-1920s.

Denver Public Library Western History Collection

poration. Ira, a noted inventor, designed and produced the Humphreys Spiral, used for the separation of gold ore.

Ruth Humphreys was the daughter of Charles Boettcher and his wife Fannie. She was born in 1890 and educated at Wolfe Hall downtown and at a private school in Philadelphia. One of the great beauties of her day, she reigned over the Silver Serpent's Ball of the Festival of Mountain and Plain of 1912. She married Humphreys in 1919 and was extremely active in social and civic work and in various philanthropies. She was an early supporter of the Denver Art Museum and made numerous donations to other causes. The Humphreys were members of the "Sacred 36," an elite group of prominent citizens headed by the formidable Mrs. Crawford Hill.

Ruth Humphreys died in 1959, and her widowed husband married again, this time to the former Mrs. Henry C. Van Schaack, a member of another prominent Denver family. Humphrey's daughter, Ruth Augusta, married D.R.C. ("Darcy") Brown, and Charline married Vic Breeden in 1955. The Breedens had three children, Holly, Vic III, and Spicer. For about fifteen years, their family lived in the Boettcher lodge on Lookout Mountain. Charline died in 1972 at the age of forty-three, and Vic Breeden died in 1998. The mountain estate is open to the public and is used as a conference center and for social events.

After the death of Albert E. Humphreys, Jr. in 1968, the Humboldt Street house changed hands a number of times. In the early 1980s, it was sold to Mr. and Mrs. O. Wesley Box. He was from western Texas, and she was a daughter of a former owner of the Shirley-Savoy Hotel in downtown Denver. The current owners, Mark and Diane Hayden, purchased the house more than ten years ago and have raised their three children there. They also managed to update and redecorate the interior, while remaining essentially true to the period. They have recently placed the property on the market.

One last tragedy brought the family names of Boettcher and Humphreys back into the spotlight. In 1996, police were hunting for the hit-and-run driver of a rare "cosmos black" BMW, a car so exotic it could be traced by its paint job. The car was the focus of a fatal accident that took the life of newspaper columnist Greg Lopez. The driver of the BMW was traveling over 100 miles per hour when it hit Lopez's car on Interstate 25 and sent him rolling across the highway. Police traced the car to Spicer Breeden, age thirty-six, grandson of Albert E. Humphreys, Jr. and great-grandson of Charles Boettcher, Sr. Breeden, who inherited a fortune from his family, had a passion for fast cars and was known to buy a new car every three or four months. Breeden was traveling that night with a friend, Lodo artist Jorg "Peter" Schmitz. It was never determined who was actually driving when the accident occurred. When police went to Breeden's house to question him, they found his body with a self-inflicted gunshot wound. He had also shot his dog.

Chapter 18

J.K. Mullen House

896 Pennsylvania Street

Architects: Aaron Gove & Thomas Walsh

Built: circa 1890

The house that John K. Mullen built at the southeast corner of Ninth Avenue. and Pennsylvania Street. was certainly as grand and expansive as those of his neighbors and business associates. His, however, was built not to impress so much as it was to host genial family gatherings that he and his wife, Katherine, treasured so much. The patriarch of an illustrious Denver family, Mullen was born in Galway, Ireland, in 1846 and came to the United States with his parents at the age of nine. The family settled in New York State. Mullen went to work for a nearby flour mill at the age of fourteen, and through diligence and hard work, he advanced to head miller at the age of twnety.

He was soon struck with wanderlust and found himself thinking of adventure in the West that he had heard so much about. He left New York and headed to Illinois, where he stayed only a few months before moving again, this time to Kansas. He came to Denver in 1871.

Mullen immediately became the manager of the Shackelton & Davis flour mill at Eighth and Curtis streets, in the Auraria neighborhood. Four years later, he and a partner formed their own milling business in north Denver. He soon bought out his partner and named the business J.K. Mullen & Company. His astute business acumen was instrumental in the rapid advancement of the company, and he soon bought up other mills in the area. In 1880, he constructed the Hungarian Elevator, the first grain elevator in Colorado, at Eighth

Ferril—Sketches of Colorado

John Kernan Mullen.

Eugene Weckbaugh, lived in a French-style house at 450 East Ninth Avenue, built in 1908 and still standing. May Dower, wife of John Dower, lived next door, at 875 Pennsylvania Street, in a house with a stately portico and finished inside with handcrafted hardwoods. It was built in 1909 and exists today. A third daughter, Edith, married Oscar Malo and moved into a palatial estate on the southeast corner of Eighth Avenue and Pennsylvania Street, adjacent to the governor's mansion. The Malo mansion is an outstanding example of the Spanish Colonial Revival style. A fourth daughter, Katherine (Mrs. John O'Connor), lived with her family at 860 Pennsylvania Street. All homes were to become social centers of Capitol Hill.

The Ella Weckbaugh house on Ninth Avenue. was a study in formal design. Each room had a distinct purpose and was to be used only as such. The dining room boasted three French mirrors, each with a hand-painted leather panel on the top. The main staircase featured four long, narrow, painted panels of flowers and birds. The house had exceptional detailing throughout, including carved woodwork and decorative plaster. The house has generally been a private residence, but for many years it was the Italian consulate.

John K. Mullen was widely known as a philanthropist who was genuinely interested in where his money went and what it went for. He financed the construction of the Mullen Home for the Aged, on West Twenty-Ninth Avenue, now the Little Sisters of the Poor. He also built the Mullen Home for Boys. The Cathedral of the Immaculate Conception benefited from many generous donations made by Mullen. In 1924, he donated $750,000 for the construction of a large library at the Catholic University in Washington, D.C. He also gave money in 1921 for the bronze statue "The Broncho Buster" in Civic Center Park, where it remains today. Mullen High School was named in his honor. He died in 1929 in his Pennsylvania Street home.

Street and Wazee. The Hungarian Flour mills were constructed in conjunction with this elevator. The business was soon expanded to surrounding states and became one of the largest such operations in the West.

Mullen didn't limit his interests to the processing of flour. He bought up cattle and invested in real estate. At one time, he was the president of five land and cattle companies in Colorado. He became chairman of the board of the Colorado Milling and Elevator Company. He also sat on the board of the Denver Public Library Association. He was a director of the First National Bank and was heavily involved in other financial institutions. A staunch Catholic, he donated large amounts of money for the construction of St. Cajetan's Church, built on the site of his former home in Auraria, and the chapel at the University of Denver. Mullen was made a Knight of the Order of Malta by Pope Pius, and in 1921, he was knighted by Pope Benedict XV.

Mullen and his wife had four daughters. As they left home to start their own families, Mullen built a mansion for each daughter nearby. Ella, wife of

The Mullens had previously lived at Ninth and Lawrence streets, in a house they subsequently donated to the Catholic church. It has been demolished. The mansion at 896 Pennsylvania

Severe in its design, the John Mullen house sat prominently on a corner site at Ninth Avenue and Pennsylvania Street.

Street remained in the family until it was converted to offices in 1953. For many years, it housed the American Humane Association. It was torn down in the 1970s, along with the former O'Connor mansion, and the property is now used for parking for the Governor's Place condos. The house at 875 Pennsylvania Street for a time was converted to apartments.

Ella Mullen Weckbaugh sold the house on East Ninth Avenue and built a palatial estate in the Country Club area on East Cedar Avenue. The home was completed in 1933. Three years earlier, her sister, Katherine O'Connor, built an equally large mansion close by, but she died before its completion. John O'Connor remained in the house for twenty years before it was sold. The sprawling Tudor-style O'Connor estate remains hidden from public view.

Mrs. Weckbaugh was a dominant force in the city's early social scene. Born in Denver in 1875, she graduated from Loretto Heights College, an institution to which she gave generously later in life, and St. Mary's Academy. During World War I, she served as women's regional chairman for the War Bond Committee.

In 1903, she married Eugene Henry Weckbaugh, and they had two children, Eleanore and J. Kernan. Mrs. Weckbaugh became president of the Mullen Benevolent Association, which oversaw the Mullen Home for the Aged and the Mullen Home for Boys.

Mrs. Weckbaugh was a generous benefactor to many organizations and institutions, among them the Katherine Mullen Memorial Home for Nurses and the Sacred Heart Chapel, both at St. Joseph Hospital; the Denver Symphony Orchestra; the Cathedral of the Immaculate Conception; the Central City Opera House Association; and the United Fund. She was also a supporter of the St. Thomas Seminary. Before she died in 1971, in her nineties, she was honored by the Catholic church as Princess of the Church for her support and philanthropy.

Mrs. Weckbaugh's daughter, Eleanore, was also a force to be reckoned with. She was smart and opinionated and didn't mince words when it came to one of her many passionate interests. A widely known art patron and philanthropist, she supported the Central City Opera House Association, the Civic Symphony (later to become the Denver Symphony), the Denver Civic Ballet Company, and the Denver Art Museum. An avid theatergoer, her after-theater parties were legendary, and attracted the best-known names in the city, as well as major

and minor celebrities from across the country. She held six major parties every year at the Cedar Avenue mansion: an open house the first Sunday after New Year's Eve, a Valentine's party with a tree decorated with flowers and red hearts, a party at Easter, a cast party for the Central City Opera, a cast party for the Elitch's Theater, and a play party for the Central City Opera.

Miss Weckbaugh attended the Wolcott School for Girls, then located at Fourteenth Avenue and Marion Street, and private schools on the East Coast. A close friend of Caroline Bancroft, local author and historian, she traveled in the highest social, musical, and literary circles and was a patron to many up-and-coming local talents.

She was also known for sending telegrams and letters and making phone calls to local officials when she felt a real or imagined slight, such as when the Cathedral of the Immaculate Conception at Colfax Avenue and Logan Street planned a major remodeling in the 1970s. She, her father, and her grandfather

The residences of May Mullen Dower (left) and Ella Mullen Weckbaugh still stand.

Author's Collection

The Ella Mullen Weckbaugh mansion, built in the manner of a French country estate, at the southern edge of the Denver Country Club.

had donated money and goods to the church over many years, and there was objection to the removal and displacement of light fixtures and a marble altar railing that the family had supplied to the church. She went so far as to request a court order to halt the remodeling project, a request that was denied by a judge. As in the case of the aforementioned objection to the razing of the Campion mansion in the 1960s, she sent letters to developers and other authorities expressing her disgust at what she perceived as the plundering of her beloved city.

When Eleanore Weckbaugh died in 1977 at the age of seventy-two, she was remembered not only for her generosity and support of the arts, but as a genuinely concerned citizen, mindful of the events shaping the city and state, yet balanced with a sense of fun and frivolity. She was buried at the Weckbaugh plot at Mount Olivet Cemetery, adjacent to that of the Mullens.

The Cedar Avenue mansion was built on a hill overlooking the Denver Country Club and Cherry Creek. Originally, the plan was for a much larger residence and was to be the home of Mrs. Myron Blackmer. Plans were scaled back and construction

began in 1930. The house, built in the French chateau style, was opened in 1933. Italian marble was used extensively throughout the house, especially in the main entrance hall and the fireplaces. The main staircase had a handwrought iron railing. The spacious drawing room was finished in eighteenth-century French style and boasted a lavender marble fireplace mantle. The artwork in this room included paintings by Boucher and Sir Joshua Reynolds. Paintings by Thomas Gainsborough and other European masters hung elsewhere in the house. Much of the furniture was from Europe, and some was especially made for the Weckbaughs. The dining room featured Austrian drapes and a ceiling of gold leaf.

Many of the rooms overlooked sweeping vistas, and the terraced gardens sloped down toward the greens of the country club. A large swimming pool, complete with its own bathhouse, was on a lower level of the back of the house. A tower at the back on the top floor featured a staircase with a ceiling that was painted blue, with metal stars depicting constellations.

The mansion was sold after Eleanore Weckbaugh's death and has changed hands since.

Chapter 19

HORACE W. BENNETT HOUSE

1300 LOGAN STREET

ARCHITECT: A. QUAYLE

BUILT: DATE UNKNOWN

The Horace W. Bennett house at the northeast corner of Thirteenth Avenue and Logan Street, was a Denver landmark for many years. The house, built in the 1880s of red Colorado sandstone, was an imposing sight, with its castellated roofline, turrets, bays, and cut-glass windows. Bennett was born in Michigan in 1862, and as a young man he heard of the money that was being made in the West. He decided to avail himself of the opportunities and settled in the Cripple Creek mining area. He made a fortune during the mining boom, but not in the usual way: instead of staking a claim, he purchased parcels of land and sold the lots at a hefty profit. When it was discovered that one of the area's greatest mines was on land that he owned, he sold out for a fortune. He came to Denver with pockets full of money and invested heavily in real estate, especially along Fifteenth Street downtown, at that time the city's business district. Not only did he sell vacant property, but he either bought or built many commercial structures in the area, in partnership with Julius Myers. Together they formed Bennett & Myers, which became one of the largest real-estate companies in the region. Along with Charles Boettcher and Henry Porter, another prominent Denver pioneer, the team invested in many major downtown properties, including the Gas & Electric Building, the Kittredge Building (still standing on Sixteenth Street), the Iron Building, and others. One of the company's largest holdings was the immense Tabor Grand Opera House, built by H.A.W. Tabor in 1880. It was located at the southwest corner of Sixteenth and Curtis streets. Bennett also

owned the St. Francis Hotel and the Ernest & Cranmer Building downtown.

Bennett had been married and widowed when he met Julie Riche, a French woman who added a sense of gaiety and charm to his life, and to whom he was devoted.

The house, designed by A. Quayle, contained twenty-two rooms, with five bedrooms on the second floor and a ballroom and servants' quarters on the top floor. A focal point of the house was the large reception hall, with a massive open staircase winding all the way to the third floor. The mansion was decorated by a celebrated New York firm, and many of the furnishings were custom made for the house. Much of the paneling was oak, as were the floors. The door hinges and knobs were bronze. The dining-room chairs were upholstered in the same pattern as appeared on the walls, and the room contained a massive built-in buffet in solid oak. Marble, tile, and porcelain were used extensively in the three bathrooms and kitchen.

In the early 1900s, the Bennetts moved to Wolhurst, a huge estate south of the city that had previously belonged to Senator Oliver Wolcott, and later to Senator Thomas Walsh, who had made his millions in mining investments.

Bennett died in 1941, and Wolhurst, which later gained notoriety as an illegal gambling and drinking club, was burned to the ground under suspicious circumstances.

David May purchased the Logan Street house from Bennett. May, who started a small retail store in Denver during the mining boom, later became prominent as a merchandising leader. His store, the May Company, later merged with Daniels and Fisher to become May D&F, one of the most well-known department stores in the state. The May Company eventually expanded into a chain. When the store's headquarters moved to the Midwest, the house was sold again, this time to Delos Chappell, who made his money mainly in public utilities. He had acquired an interest in Trinidad's First National Bank and became involved in the development of the coal industry there. He expanded his investments to include the Victor Fuel Company and moved those offices to Denver. He was also elected president of the Nevada California Electric Company and the Hydro-Electric Company, which furnished power to Southern California and parts of Nevada.

Chappell and his wife, May, had two children, Delos Jr. and Jean Louise, who later became Mrs. George Cranmer. In 1898, the family moved to Denver from Trinidad, where Chappell had been busy laying out the city's water system. They lived for a time in a stone house at the corner of Colfax Avenue and Race Street and later moved to 1555 Race Street. In 1905, when Jean had graduated from finishing school, the family went abroad for two years, touring Europe, as Chappell travelled back and forth to Denver to keep an eye on his business interests. It was on one of those visits he decided to purchase the Logan Street house from David May.

The family took possession in 1907, and the house immediately became a center for social and musical events. Both Mrs. Chappell, who was an accomplished artist, and Jean, who was a trained musician, had a keen interest in the arts. The two became patrons to many talented locals, many of whom went on to national and international prominence. Jean had met George Cranmer while ice skating at City Park lake. They were soon married, and the couple joined the parents in the Logan Street house.

Jean Cranmer opened the house to some of the most brilliant and memorable parties of the day. She was heavily involved in charity work and was one of the foremost patrons of the arts in the city. She founded the Friends of Chamber Music and the Allied Arts Organization, and she was the first president of the Denver Symphony Society. She also helped to found the Aspen Music School.

In 1922, after the death of Delos Chappell, the house was presented by his children to the Denver Art Association. It later became the home of the Indian collection of the Denver Art Museum.

The city of Denver and the state of Colorado have much to be thankful for because of the vision and

The George Cranmer residence at 200 Cherry Street.

dedication of George E. Cranmer. During the 1920s and 1930s, Cranmer was a driving force in helping to greatly expand the parks system. As parks manager, Cranmer was responsible for overseeing the vast acreage of forests, rivers, lakes, and campsites that were a big tourist draw in Colorado and a huge source of revenue for the state coffers. He was responsible, for the most part, for the planning and development of Red Rocks Amphitheater and the Winter Park Ski Resort.

Cranmer was born in Denver. He was an avid outdoorsman from an early age and spent time on his uncle's ranch in Wyoming as a young boy. He had a deep respect for the land and considered Colorado one of the most beautiful places in the country.

After he graduated from Princeton, he became a stockbroker and made a fortune before pulling out immediately before the Crash of 1929. His timing, as in all things, was perfect.

Cranmer gained his position as parks manager in the mid-1930s as a result of his campaign efforts on behalf of Benjamin Stapleton, Denver mayor from

1923 to 1931 and again from 1935 to 1947, when he was replaced by Quigg Newton.

George and Jean Cranmer moved to east Denver in 1917. Their house, designed by Jacques Benedict in a low Italianate style, was far out in the country at the time it was constructed. The house, at 200 Cherry Street, was built in a U-shape with a courtyard in the center. The great drawing room, with its vaulted ceiling and French doors, was the center of the house, drawing together the many personages that availed themselves of the Cranmer's hospitality. A huge Aubusson carpet covered the floor, and the room was filled with art collected by the Cranmers during their world travels.

The author was a visitor to the home as a child and remembers Mrs. Cranmer recalling one of her most famous charity events, the "circus party." In the late 1930s, the grounds were elaborately decorated to resemble a circus sideshow, and the swimming pool to the back of the mansion was surrounded by Chinese lanterns. Guests were encouraged to try their luck at the shooting gallery, and for ten cents they could vent their frustrations by smashing china and pottery

against a stone wall. A buffet dinner followed, with dancing later on a specially built dance floor on the lower terrace.

The house was visited by many famous people, including Frank Lloyd Wright, Josef and Rosina Lhevinne, Sergei Prokoviev (the Russian composer), Mischa Elman, Antonia Brico (the eccentric female conductor), and the cast members of many of the visiting road shows. The Cranmers remained in the house until the 1960s. It is still privately owned.

Although Wolhurst, the second Horace Bennett home, was built south of Denver on the Arapahoe/ Douglas County lines, it is included here not only because of its ties to many prominent Denver families but because of its illustrious visitors and sordid history. Wolhurst was built originally as a country home by Senator Edward Wolcott, who wanted a place where he could get away from the pressures of his business and political life. He purchased 400 acres at 8101 South Santa Fe Drive. Wolcott's love of the open spaces brought him here, where he could enjoy the serenity and unobstructed view of the Colorado

Rockies. He and his wife settled at Wolhurst after their large, Tudor-style house, designed by architect Theodore Boal, was finished in the 1890s. They soon found the house inadequate for Mrs. Wolcott's entertaining and added a number of large rooms until the total was around twenty five. The floor plan of the house wrapped tightly around the crescent-shaped drive to the entrance. The house had a large drawing room, a library, numerous bedrooms, a large kitchen, and enclosed porches. The rooms were furnished in typical plush Victorian style, and the house offered its visitors a very comfortable and inviting place to stay.

While the Wolcotts were in ownership, a number of important business and political people were guests, including British nobility, Russian aristocracy, and European diplomats. The Wolcotts entertained in grand style, and the rambling house was usually filled with people. The pressures of Wolcott's career, however, made deep inroads on his marriage, and the couple divorced in 1900. Mrs. Wolcott moved out, and a year later the senator decided to add on to the already sprawling house by building a sunroom com-

Wolhurst, the rambling estate of Senator Edward Wolcott in south Denver.

Denver Public Library Western History Collection

plete with an octagonal tower. In lieu of his wife's absence, entertaining was taken care of by Wolcott's sister, Anna Wolcott, who was headmistress of the Wolcott School for Girls at Fourteenth Avenue and Marion Street. The senator, however, began spending less and less time at the house and died in his fifties in 1905 in Monte Carlo, thousands of miles away from his beloved Colorado.

The next owner was the colorful Thomas Walsh, who made millions in the mines of Colorado and elsewhere. Walsh and his wife made numerous changes to the property, including enlarging the house even further, to a total of fifty-one rooms, and altering the landscaping. Ponds and fountains were added to the already lush surroundings.

Walsh had political aspirations that ran deep, and he mingled with the top politicians of both Colorado and Washington. Political luminaries who were guests of the Walshes included President Taft, Vice-President Fairbanks, and Alice Roosevelt Longworth, irreverent daughter of President Theodore Roosevelt. Longworth was a great friend of the Walshes' flamboyant daughter, Evalyn, a tomboy who, as Evalyn Walsh McLean, evolved into one of Washington's leading hostesses. She also became

the owner of the world-famous (and supposedly cursed) Hope diamond and the fabled Star of the East. She generously opened her Washington estate to hundreds of servicemen during the Second World War and let, to their astonishment, her dog roam the rooms of the great house wearing the world's most valuable blue diamond around his neck.

With the Walshes spending more time in Washington and Newport, it was decided to put Wolhurst up for sale. This time it was purchased by the Horace Bennetts, who owned the estate from 1910 to 1944. Horace Bennett had made a fortune in real estate and was considered one of the foremost speculators in the West. The social scene at Wolhurst continued unabated during the Bennetts' residency. It was the scene of their daughter's elaborate wedding, noted in every newspaper of the day. The Bennetts sold the estate, and the property went to Frank Kistler, Oklahoma oilman. He spent so little time on the property that it was soon sold back to the Bennetts at cost. It was around this time that the first of three questionable fires broke out on the property, destroying a number of outbuildings and doing minor damage to the main house.

Horace Bennett died in 1941, and Mrs. Bennett sold the acreage in 1944 to Charlie Stephens, a dubious character who had a shady past and a number of aliases. She was under the impression that he would open the house as a "fine restaurant and social club" and felt secure that her former house would be well taken care of. Stephens and his cousin, Edward Jordan, converted the estate into one of Colorado's most notorious gambling clubs, one that attracted the well-heeled and seasoned gamblers from all points. Renamed the Wolhurst Saddle Club, it did, indeed, offer horseback riding, swimming, and other outdoor activities. But the main draws were the gambling tables inside—dice games, poker, slots, and roulette. The crowds kept coming, and all the while the authorities turned a blind eye, even after many complaints had been made to the city concerning troubles at the estate.

The whole city of Denver turned its attention on Wolhurst, however, when, in 1946, thirteen masked men pulled up in front of the house, entered

The interior of Wolhurst at the time of Horace Bennett's ownership.

through the front door, and ordered everyone in the house at gunpoint to surrender their cash, jewels, and other valuables. The thieves made off with a reported $100,000, although that figure was later amended to a lesser amount. The matter was a huge embarrassment to those present and was kept as hushed up as possible due to some of the prominent names involved. Those responsible for the holdup were never caught.

Trouble didn't stop there. In February 1951, a disastrous fire raced through the structure, killing two people and causing major damage to the estate. The cause of the fire was suspicious, and fingers pointed to everyone from disgruntled gamblers to members of the mob. The only part of the house left undamaged was the sunroom. Plans were made to rebuild, although on a smaller scale, and operations were soon back to what they had been previously. But trouble continued to shadow the place.

The house was raided in 1958, and fourteen men were jailed on vice charges. The house had been raided a number of times before but with disappointing results. This raid centered on a stag party being given by a group of businessmen and featured not only gambling, but strippers as well.

The operation finally settled into a legitimate enterprise when it was opened as the Wolhurst Country Club. It remained in operation until a third fire in 1976 completely burned down the structure. By this time, most of the surrounding property had been sold off for a trailer park, and the manor house sat on only eight acres.

There is little left, save the neighborhood tag "Wolhurst," to give evidence of the illustrious and famed history of the area.

Chapter 20

WILLIAM BERGER HOUSE

1170 SHERMAN STREET

ARCHITECT: UNKNOWN

BUILT: 1881

I n the last quarter of the nineteenth century, Denver's three avenues of distinction were Grant Street, Sherman Street, and Colfax Avenue. It's difficult to imagine today that these streets were once lined on both sides with massive Victorian dwellings boasting towers, turrets, cupolas, verandas, widow's walks, iron fencing, stone walls, and sweeping, manicured lawns, complete with a retinue of loyal help. Henry C. Brown had obtained a tract that was broken into lots, known as Brown's Second Addition. The William B. Berger house was one of the first to be built in that area, located near the southeast corner of Twelfth and Sherman streets. Originally designed as a large, red-brick house fronting Sherman Street with a back stable, a later addition connected the two to make one sprawling residence. The property took up approximately seven lots. William B. Berger built this house for himself and his wife, the former Margaret Kountze, and their six children. William Berger was born in Pittsburgh, Pennsylvania, in 1839. After studying there and abroad, he came West in 1869 in search of a cure for his asthma. Stopping in Cheyenne, Wyoming, he quickly found employment with the banking firm of Kountze Brothers and Company. He soon rose in position there and was sent to Denver in 1872 to work with the Kountze concern, the Colorado National Bank. Berger became a manager and stockholder of that institution. He was also one of the principal founders of the Struby-Estabrook Mercantile Company, in a building that is still extant close to Union Station on Seventeenth Street. Berger also was a stockholder in the Globe Smelting Company and held stock in

The William Berger mansion is now the site of twin apartment houses.

various other companies, including mining and railroading. Berger was treasurer of Denver School District #1. He died after a brief illness in March 1890. His widow continued to live in the Sherman Street house until her death in 1922.

Their children continued in the banking business. One son in particular, William Bart Berger, carried on the family involvement with Colorado National Bank and rose through the ranks to become vice-president, in the tradition of his father and his uncle, Charles B. Kountze. The Kountze family were early pioneers in finance in the state. In 1898, William Bart Berger married Ethel Sayre, daughter of Hal Sayre, whose unusual Moorish-style house still stands adjacent to the Governor's Mansion on Eighth Avenue and Logan Street. William Bart Berger had a white brick residence at 765 Pennsylvania Street, and built a large greenhouse next door to raise his prized orchids, a hobby for which he was known throughout the state. He moved from there to his new showplace at 2925 East Exposition Avenue, in the Polo Grounds area, in 1929, and died in 1931. His Pennsylvania Street mansion was wrecked in the early 1960s. The site is now occupied by Governor's Park.

After Margaret Berger's death, the Lamont School of Music, directed by Florence Lamont Hinman, moved into the Sherman Street house, and it was used as a music conservatory until 1941, when the Lamont School moved into the former home of John Sidney Brown, at 909 Grant Street. The Berger house was leveled the following year to make way for modern twin apartment buildings of blond brick in a modified streamline style at 1160 and 1180 Sherman Street. The apartments and the original low-rise retaining wall that ran around most of the Berger property still stand today.

The Bergers eventually had a close neighbor, William Fullerton, who was to build his residence at 1200 Sherman Street in 1888. Fullerton was a director of the First National Bank and was also a mine owner. He moved his large family into the house, which featured large, airy rooms and a large stable in the back of the property. The family retained ownership of the house even after Mr. Fullerton's death, and his widow lived there until 1947, when she died at the age of ninety. Her neighbor to the immediate east, Fannie Boettcher, also lived in her massive residence until her death in 1952, at which time the two houses were summarily wrecked for the new Colorado Department of Employment Building, which is still in use today. Mrs. Fullerton and Mrs. Boettcher were two of the last surviving family members to retain ownership of their original Capitol Hill mansions. Most had passed out of family hands well before then.

At the southwest corner of Twelfth Avenue and Grant Street sat the Edward Eddy mansion, built in the 1880s. Eddy was a director of the Grant Smelter, operating at that time in north Denver. The house, built of stone and brick with a large veranda and an imposing tower, passed from the Eddys to the Whitney Newtons, the forebearers of Quigg Newton, Denver mayor in the late 1940s. The house was torn down in 1940, and Central Business College was built on the site. That building still stands.

The Eddy mansion at Twelfth Avenue and Grant Street, later the site of Central Business College.

Chapter 21

J.J. and Molly Brown House

1340 Pennsylvania Street

Architect: William Lang

Built: 1889–90

Probably no other name is as closely associated with Colorado's colorful history than that of Margaret "Molly" Brown. She was born Margaret Tobin in Hannibal, Missouri, in 1867, daughter of a hard-working laborer and his wife. The family was poor and devoutly religious. Margaret had always dreamed of a way out of her drab surroundings, and at the young age of fifteen, she followed her brother to Colorado, where he had heard of the many who were making piles of money in the gold and silver mines of Leadville. There they settled, and she fell into the routine of dutiful caretaker to her brother while he toiled in the mines searching for riches.

While in Leadville, Margaret met James J. Brown, who, at that time, had not had much success prospecting but was making a good living as a mine supervisor. James J. Brown had joined the legions of men who were lured by the promise of riches in the Black Hills of South Dakota in 1877. After scant success, he followed other prospectors out to Colorado in 1879.

While Molly had her eye out for a rich catch, something about J.J. sparked a flame. The two were soon married, and she faced the prospect that she may end up as nothing more than the wife of a relatively successful supervisor.

That all changed, of course, when J.J. and his partners, among them John Campion and Eben Smith, made a huge strike at the

Denver Public Library Western History Collection

Margaret "Molly" Brown.

group of elitists would have meant Molly had finally "arrived."

Molly was never completely ostracized from Denver society. She was looked upon as a curiosity. She cultivated her own circle of friends, although she was not able to break into "real" Denver society, an ever-present reminder of her origins, and it was a constant frustration throughout most of her life. Many doors were still closed to her. She found acceptance elsewhere—in the East Coast circles and abroad, especially in Paris. In actuality, she led a life pretty close to that of most society matrons of the time. She lived in style in the grand house that her husband bought for her on Pennsylvania Street, she had hired help, and she sent her son and daughter to the best schools. Her manner was peculiar, however; she was a flashy dresser and spoke in a brash tone, although she was probably not as brassy as she has been portrayed in print and in motion pictures.

She will be forever linked to the sinking of the great liner *Titanic*. As a passenger aboard the ill-fated ship, there was virtually nothing to foretell of the events that were to unfold on the clear, cold night of April 14, 1912—events that would change her life.

CHRONOLOGY OF EVENTS OF APRIL 1912

APRIL 10—*Titanic* starts its maiden voyage from Southampton, England, to New York.

APRIL 14—Sends a routine wireless warning ashore of the presence of icebergs off the Grand Banks of Newfoundland.

APRIL 14—11:40 P.M., *Titanic* strikes an iceberg in latitude 41.16 north, longitude 50.14 west.

APRIL 14—Midnight, *Carpathia* and other vessels hear *Titanic*'s call for help.

APRIL 15—12:27 A.M., *Titanic*'s wireless is put out of commission and flashes are given that the boat is sinking by the head, and women and children are being put off in lifeboats.

APRIL 15—2:20 A.M., *Titanic* sinks.

Little Jonny Mine, which was part of the Ibex Mine Company. Money shot out of it like a geyser.

Even with a fabulous fortune to back her, Molly's attempts to enter Denver society were met with continued frustration. The times were different then: it didn't matter as much that you were accomplished or educated or rich; it only really mattered where you came from and who your family was. It was smug and pretentious—and widely accepted.

J.J. and Molly, of course, had no prominent forebears that they could name, and the fact that J.J. struck it rich in the hills above Denver still did not count much to the cloistered inner circles of Denver society, which was ruled almost single-handedly by Mrs. Crawford Hill. Mrs. Hill's white palace, at Tenth Avenue and Sherman Street, was the center of the universe to those lucky enough to be included in her set—the "Sacred 36." This group, Denver's answer to Caroline Astor's New York "Four Hundred," was comprised of the upper echelon of Denver's power brokers and their wives. Belonging to this

APRIL 15—5 A.M., first survivors picked up from lifeboats by steamer *Carpathia.*

APRIL 15—Noon, reports that *Titanic* still afloat and that all are saved.

APRIL 16—*Carpathia* sends by wireless list of survivors, failing to account for about 1,300 persons, including scores of wealthy and prominent people.

APRIL 18—Two days elapsed without slightest description of disaster.

APRIL 18—9:30 P.M., rescue ship docks at New York with 705 passengers and crew of the original 2,227 passengers, confirming the loss of all others and bringing the first details of the *Titanic* disaster.

It is practically impossible to imagine, in this age of instant news and worldwide media, that reports of the disaster were slow in coming, sporadic, and inaccurate. Days elapsed between the actual event and news of the scope of the disaster and numbers of lives lost.

Lady Duff Gordon, interviewed shortly after the disaster, gave her own account to reporters:

I was asleep. The night was perfectly clear. I was awakened by a long grinding sort of shock. It was not a tremendous crash, but more as though someone had drawn a giant finger all along the side of the boat. I awakened my husband, Sir Cosmo, and told him that I thought that we had struck something.

My husband went on deck and told me that we had hit an iceberg but there seemed to be little danger. We were shortly told to put our clothes on as orders had been given to strip the boats. We each put on a life preserver and over mine I threw some heavy furs. We went up on deck, and there was no great excitement at the time. The ship has listed slightly to port and was down a little at the head. As we stood there, one of the officers came rushing up and said: "The

women and children are to go into the boats." No one apparently thought there was any danger.

We watched a number of women and children and some men climb into the lifeboats. An officer came to me and told me I had better get into a boat. The boat was the twelfth or thirteenth to be launched. Five stokers got in and two Americans. Besides these there were two of the crew, Sir Cosmo, myself, and a Miss Frank, an English girl.

There were a number of other passengers standing nearby, and they joked with us because we were going out to sea. "The ship can't sink," they said. "You will get your death of cold out there in the ice." We began to row away and for two hours we cruised around. It did not seem very cold. There was no excitement aboard the *Titanic.* We were probably a mile away.

Almost immediately we heard several pistol shots and a great screaming arising from the decks. Then the boat's stern lifted in the air and there was a tremendous explosion. After this the *Titanic* dropped back again. The awful screaming continued. Two minutes after this there was another great explosion. The whole forward part of the great liner dropped down under the waves. The stern rose a hundred feet almost perpendicularly. The boat stood up like an enormous black finger against the sky. Little figures hung to the point of the finger and dropped into the water. The screaming was agonizing.

The great prow of the *Titanic* slowly sank as though a great hand was pushing it gently down under the waves. As it went down, the screaming of the poor souls left on board seemed to grow louder. It took the *Titanic* perhaps two minutes to sink after the last explosion. It went down slowly without a ripple.

The Molly Brown house at 1340 Pennsylvania Street.

Author's Collection

Many of those lost were steerage passengers. Most liners at the time supported themselves through steerage fares, as thousands of people were then emigrating to America and Canada. First class did not have the volume of passengers to pay to keep the great ships running. Most in steerage were kept deep in the bowels of the boat.

Molly gained her worldwide fame partly through her own heroic efforts and partly through an ever-growing media myth. It was known, and reported later, that she took charge of her boat. She did what she could to quell the hysteria and made everyone row, even the weakest aboard, away from the great ship and away from harm's way. It was also reported that, after being picked up with the rest by the *Carpathia*, she nursed many of the victims in the ship's hospital and saw to their needs even through her own great despair and exhaustion.

Molly herself gave this account to a *Denver Post* reporter just a week after the catastrophe:

> There, in that lifeboat, with a sailor at my side, I rowed for all my might for seven and a half hours. I rowed until my head was sick, until I thought I was dead. Fifteen more could have been saved in our boat.

> I owe my life to my exercise. Two women died at my side of exposure, while my blood was at a boiling point. You can imagine the shouting and crying that went up when the *Carpathia* came to us out of the misty daylight.

> Two hours after that I was in the ship's hospital, nursing the hysterical. Don't ask me how I did it—I don't know myself.

Molly Brown returned to Denver a true heroine, and she basked in the glow of publicity. She was the star of the hour.

Mrs. Crawford Hill, who had done much to keep Molly out of the true inner circles of Denver society, actually relented once, and only once. She held a luncheon in Molly's honor at the Denver Country Club. Molly never was admitted as a member of Denver's Sacred 36.

J.J. Brown never shared Molly's aspirations and found it all very boring. The couple grew apart and finally separated. Molly filled her time with traveling and spent more and more time away from Denver. The Pennsylvania Street house was rented over the next few years, and Molly spent most of her time at her home in Newport, Rhode Island, and in Europe.

J.J. Brown died in 1922, and Molly died in New York a decade later. She is buried in Long Island.

The mansion was converted to apartments and later to a boardinghouse. In the mid-1960s, it became a center for delinquent girls, run by the juvenile courts. During this time, the house was in a state of decay, as were a majority of the mansions in Capitol Hill that had not already been torn down. It seemed that a similar fate awaited the aging house, and by this time, splinter groups of preservationists had been mulling its plight. So much of the area's history and heritage had been turned to dust that it was felt a push had to be made to save this one icon of Denver's rich past.

Partly as a result, Historic Denver, Inc. was born, and through its efforts, the house was saved for posterity. Since the early 1970s, it has been sensitively restored and operated as a popular museum and tourist destination.

Chapter 22

CRAWFORD HILL HOUSE

150 East Tenth Avenue

Architect: Theodore Boal

Built: 1904–1905

Mrs. Crawford Hill reigned supreme over the social scene of Denver's early days. Anybody who was anybody crossed the threshold of her stately white mansion at Tenth Avenue and Sherman Street. As the head of the city's "Sacred 36," comprised of the upper echelon of the city's leading citizens, she was their absolute arbiter of fashion and good taste. She attained this position by bucking earlier trends of stifling formality and convention. She was known for her elaborate all-night parties and for furnishing popular music at her functions, as opposed to the strictly conventional classical venues offered by other hostesses. Extreme wealth was not an automatic invitation into her inner circle. One had to have a "background." She had little use for the nouveau riche of her day. She remained ensconced on her throne for three decades before acceding to changing times and attitudes.

Her husband, son of U.S. Senator Nathaniel Hill, was a force in his own right. Born in 1862, he received his early education at Black Hawk before attending college back East. Upon his return, he went to work for the *Denver Republican* newspaper, which was owned by his father. He soon branched out into other business ventures, including real estate, mining and smelting, oil, communications, and banking. Hill became president of the Denargo Land Company and the Hill Land and Investment Company, and he was a director of the Boston Smelting Company and the Continental Tunnel Railway Company. He also was a director of the Denver YWCA and the Museum of

Natural History and was chairman of the Republican National Convention in Chicago in 1908.

Louise Hill, nee Sneed, came from an aristocratic family from Tennessee. She married Crawford Hill in 1895, and they moved from their home at 1407 Cleveland Place downtown to their Sherman Street palace in 1905. The house, designed by architect Theodore Boal, contained twenty-two rooms in three stories, plus a basement. Mrs. Hill had wanted a light and airy interior, unlike the dark, drab, cluttered Victorian rooms she had left behind her. Consequently, the walls were painted white or light gray. The large main-floor rooms were clustered off the main reception hall, with its floor of black and white Tennessee marble. The sixty-four-foot drawing room was decorated in the French Renaissance style, and most of the rooms were furnished in muted gold, ivory, and gray. Mrs. Hill's bedroom was decorated in ivory and gold, and her bed was on a raised platform in the middle of the room. All the rooms, upstairs and downstairs, were lighted with crystal chandeliers. A solarium of white marble was added to the house for a visit by then-President Taft. Other notables to visit the house were the Duke of Abruzzi, the Queen of Belgium, and Evalyn Walsh McLean, owner of the Hope diamond.

Crawford Hill died in 1922, and his widow continued to reign from her palace, playing hostess to the famous of her day. She was presented at the Court of King Edward VII.

Eventually, Mrs. Hill's spotlight faded. By the start of the Second World War, she was induced to give up her mansion for lack of help and rising costs. She

Exterior of the Crawford Hill residence on Tenth Avenue and Sherman Street.
Author's Collection

Southern exterior of the Hill mansion.

took a suite of rooms at the Brown Palace Hotel, where she lived until her death in 1955, well into her nineties.

After she moved out, the mansion sat vacant for a period. It was purchased by the Town Club in 1947. It was extensively remodeled for use as a gathering place for Jewish professionals. A swimming pool replaced Mrs. Hill's formal gardens to the south of the house. Much of the furniture was sold, and the rooms were remodeled for club use. The dining room was converted to a cocktail lounge, and the solarium was made into the club's dining room. Upstairs bedrooms were redone as card rooms. The circular drive at the entrance of the mansion was covered over and the huge iron gates closed for good. The club remained in service until the early 1980s, when the house was sold to a group of attorneys. Today it houses offices.

Mrs. Crawford Hill.

DONALD FLETCHER HOUSE

1575 GRANT STREET

ARCHITECT: UNKNOWN

BUILT: CIRCA 1888

The urban restructuring of the 1960s was not kind to two well-known Denver mansions, those of Donald Fletcher and Charles Kountze. The Fletcher mansion, which sat on the southwest corner of Sixteenth Avenue and Grant Street, was built in 1892 of red Colorado sandstone. Donald Fletcher had come to Denver, like so many others before him, to find relief from his tuberculosis. Once here, he involved himself deeply in the development of local real estate and became one of the city's foremost property owners. He also served on the board of the Chamber of Commerce and helped develop the land east of the city that eventually became Aurora. To show off his status in the community in a proper fashion, Fletcher constructed his huge residence along the very fashionable Grant Street, where others of his same circle had previously built theirs.

The house, built in the so-called Italian style of red sandstone, contained twenty-two rooms. The main floor had oak flooring and consisted of a large reception hall, a drawing room, an oak-paneled library, a dining room, a kitchen and a pantry, and a sitting room, all furnished in the typical style of the day. There were thick Persian carpets, heavy draperies, and paintings and statuary throughout the house. A conservatory was built of cherry wood and was used alternately as a sunroom and a botanic room. Fletcher had a long art gallery added to the south of the residence to house his prized collection of European paintings.

The Donald Fletcher house at 1575 Grant Street.

The second floor contained eight bedrooms, with woodwork either of cherry or mahogany, and four large bathrooms built of tile and marble. The third floor was used as servants' quarters and also contained a ballroom with a full theater stage, used for musicals and theatricals. A bowling alley was located in the basement, as well as a large swimming pool, a heating plant, and a ventilation system. The grounds stretched almost 100 feet along Grant Street, and gardeners kept the lawn, trees, and shrubs highly manicured. The large stables housed a servants' quarters as well.

Fletcher lost a great deal of money in the Silver Panic of 1893, and he left the city soon after. The house had many subsequent owners, including Colonel William Hughes and Frank Hearne. It also saw duty for a few years as a music academy. It was purchased in 1919 by the Knights of Columbus fraternal organization, who used the premises for the next four decades. In 1961, the decision was made to tear down the mansion with plans to build a large office building. The house was demolished, but the office building never came to realization. The land is now used as a parking lot. The former art gallery was left standing, and, although it is somewhat altered from its original form, it can be seen today. The Knights of Columbus still have offices directly to the south at 1555 Grant Street.

The former art gallery is all that remains of the Fletcher mansion.

Chapter 24

CHARLES KOUNTZE HOUSE

1613 GRANT STREET

ARCHITECT: A.W. FULLER

BUILT: 1882–1883

The Charles Kountze mansion, adjacent to the Fletcher residence, was one of Capitol Hill's earliest and grandest houses. The Kountze brothers—Charles, Herman, August, and Luther—were all Colorado pioneers in finance and real estate.

Charles Kountze was born in 1844 in Ohio, and by 1855, the older brothers, August and Herman, had already involved themselves in the banking business. Charles came to Denver in 1864 and settled in Central City, where he opened a bank. In 1865, he joined his brother Luther in Denver and together they formed the Kountze Brothers Bank in downtown, between Fifteenth and Sixteenth streets, and Blake Street. In 1866, the Kountze brothers organized the Colorado National Bank, and in 1871 Charles became president, serving until his death in 1911. He also served as city treasurer from 1868 to 1871. Aside from banking and large real-estate holdings, he involved himself with the building of railroads, principally the Denver, Texas & Ft. Worth and the Denver, South Park & Pacific. He also had investments in the Globe smelter.

Charles Kountze built his massive, gray-stone mansion in 1882 and spared no expense in the construction. From the start, the forty-two-room palace was meant to be a pace-setter among the monied class, and many of Kountze's cronies followed his lead by building their own versions of his western Utopia elsewhere in the neighborhood. The house was built on part of Brown's Bluff, Henry C. Brown's

Denver Public Library Western History Collection

Charles Kountze built one of the earliest, and largest, mansions in Capitol Hill, setting the pace for others behind him.

original homestead. Brown was the builder of the Brown Palace Hotel and had a home nearby close to Sixteenth Avenue and Lincoln Street.

Constructed of sandstone with walls two feet thick, Kountze's house was spacious on the inside with wide hallways and high ceilings. The main hallway had a ceiling of polished redwood and a specially made brass chandelier, originally built for gas and later electrified. The large library was wood paneled with hand-carved decorations above the ten-foot-high doors. The dining room held a generous fireplace with built-in benches on both sides and contained a built-in buffet with a marble top. An art gallery displayed the family's prized collection of paintings, and the wide stairwell leading to the upper floors boasted a huge stained-glass window on the landing. The second floor contained eight bedrooms

of generous proportions, and the top floor originally had a ballroom with a domed ceiling. Light filtered through the custom-made stained-glass windows.

Charles Kountze loved to work outdoors, and he often joined his gardeners in their work, discussing events of the day while pruning his prized rose bushes or planning that years plantings.

After his death in 1911, the family gave up the mansion and it was remodeled for use as a boardinghouse. One of Kountze's former partners, Tom Daly, had founded the highly successful Capitol Life Insurance Company, with offices in the Tabor Building on Sixteenth Street in downtown Denver. The first board of directors included Charles Boettcher, Frederick Bonfils, John Campion, Charles Hughes, Julius Myers, Eben Smith, and Adolph Zang. In

1923, Daly's son, Clarence, who had joined his father in the business, built a new headquarters building at the northeast corner of Sixteenth Avenue and Sherman Street. The imposing structure, designed by local architect Harry Manning, was constructed of Colorado white marble, which was meant to be a symbol of the business's strength and permanence. Some years later, Capitol Life purchased the Kountze estate with the intention of razing the structure. This plan was forestalled, and the mansion came into use for additional offices and storage.

In 1963, the mansion was unceremoniously wrecked to make way for an eleven-story addition to the Capitol Life Building. Capitol Life was sold in the 1980s, and the two adjoining buildings are now used for various offices.

Main stairway of the Charles Kountze mansion.

Denver Public Library Western History Collection

Chapter 25

EDWIN B. HENDRIE HOUSE

930 WASHINGTON STREET

ARCHITECT: UNKNOWN

BUILT: 1891

O f the thousands who drive by this house every week, most pay scant attention to it, if any at all. It is easily missed, as it is nestled gently among the trees and is situated unobtrusively. The builder of the house was Archibald Brownlee, mining engineer, who spent only a few years on the property before selling to Edwin B. Hendrie. Its history is as interesting as that of any on Capitol Hill. Hendrie had a long career in business and mining in Colorado. He was born in Burlington, Iowa, in 1847. He attended technical school in Philadelphia and graduated from the Polytechnic College of Pennsylvania. Hendrie came to Colorado in 1867 as an agent for his father, Charles Hendrie, who was the owner of a machinery-manufacturing plant in Burlington, Iowa, that made steamboat and railroad engines and rails for the Chicago, Burlington & Quincy Railroad.

During the Central City gold rush, Charles Hendrie came West to survey the situation. Conditions were such that he started manufacturing newer and more efficient milling machines and shipping them to the Rockies from Iowa. Soon, the Burlington machine shops were operating at capacity, and the Hendrie Company became the only manufacturer of mining machinery east of Colorado.

As the mining boom continued, Charles Hendrie spent considerable time in Central City and established a foundry and

The Edwin B. Hendrie house at 930 Washington Street.

machine shop there. While this venture occupied his time, he placed two of his three sons in charge of the Burlington shops. And as his Colorado operations expanded further, he sent for his sons to come West to help out.

Soon, Henry Bolthoff, superintendent of the Burlington shops, came West also. In 1874, Bolthoff and the two Hendrie sons, Charles and William, formed a partnership and began development of new and more efficient mining machinery, along with other products. Two years later, they opened a manufacturing business in lower downtown Denver, which was rapidly becoming the central point of commerce in the region. By the 1880s, practically all of the company's business was centered in Denver, and the company moved its main headquarters here.

In 1882, the third son, Edwin B., joined the company. The Hendrie & Bolthoff Manufacturing & Supply Company became wildly successful and shipped its increasingly diverse products nationwide.

It also exported overseas. It was, at one time, the largest company of its kind in the world. The main building was located at Seventeenth and Wynkoop streets, adjacent to Union Station, and still stands today.

Hendrie lived in his house on Washington Street through the early years of his success. In 1903, the house was sold to John W. Springer, banker and president of the Continental Trust Company, located at Sixteenth and Lawrence streets. Springer's wife, the flamboyant Isabel Patterson Springer, was one of the great beauties of her day. The Springers were considered to be respectable citizens who moved quietly in the circles of Denver society. There was nothing to indicate anything was wrong.

On the evening of May 24, 1911, in the crowded bar of the Brown Palace Hotel, Frank Henwood elbowed his way over to Tony Von Phul, who was seated at the bar having a drink, and an argument ensued. Von Phul stood up and knocked Henwood to the floor.

Henwood got up on one knee, pulled out a .38, and started shooting. Three shots hit Von Phul. Another bullet struck G.E. Copeland, a businessman visiting from Victor, Colorado, and another bullet hit J.W. Atkinson, from Colorado Springs. Blood splattered everywhere. Customers scattered.

Von Phul died shortly afterward in the hospital. Copeland died a week later from complications. Henwood went on trial, not for the murder of Von Phul, but for the death of Copeland. As the trial unfolded, it became apparent that Isabel Springer had carried on a liaison with not only Henwood,

The interior of the Hendrie house shows intricate woodwork that remains in place today.

Author's Collection

but with Von Phul as well, much to the shock of her unsuspecting husband. Letters from Von Phul to Mrs. Springer were produced, confirming their illicit affair. It was the crime of the decade, and the high-placed scandal shook Denver society to its core. Henwood was found guilty of first-degree murder and sentenced to life in prison. On appeal, a second trial was granted, and again Henwood was judged guilty, but this time was sentenced to death. After a decade in prison, Henwood was pardoned. He was imprisoned again for parole violation and died at Cañon City in 1930.

John Springer filed for, and was granted, a divorce. He sold the house on Washington Street and built a fine gray-stone house on Denver's west side, at 1655 Vrain Street, which later became an apartment house.

Isabel Springer moved to Chicago for a few years and then went on to New York, where she became a model, of sorts, and a bit player in silent films. She died in 1918 at the age of thirty-seven in a pauper's hospital from alcohol and morphine addiction.

The house at 930 Washington next became the Green Tea Inn, which catered to a middle-class clientele. An advertisement of 1924 boasted: "Lovely suites, good eats, couples or adult families, also table board." It offered a quiet haven to its guests, a country atmosphere in the heart of the city. It was also rumored at the time to have been operated as a front for a gambling house, a rumor that was never substantiated.

In 1926, the property was purchased by B. Abbott Frye, a railroad man who later became a successful building contractor and mortgage investor. By the late 1920s, the mansion was extensively remodeled and turned into the Frye Apartments, which continue to this day. The integrity of the house has been kept intact, and much of the original woodwork remains in place. Frye's daughter, Irene Gay, moved to the house with her family as a young girl and remembers it well. "The porches were already screened in, but not winterized," she said. "That was done later when the house was converted for apartments. The house had nineteen or twenty rooms originally and now

Author's Collection

The former stables at 930 Washington Street.

has fifty. There was a large recreation room on the third floor, large enough to have parties. My father added the top floor. The carriage house was put up in 1904, along with the carport." She also remembers some other changes. "There were big iron gates at the entrance and at the driveway. Both have been taken off."

Irene Gay moved out of the house in 1970, "reluctantly," she said. "I remember the house as having a great deal of charm." It has been in the same family for more than seventy years.

When Edwin Hendrie sold the Washington Street mansion, he purchased the fabled Richtofen Castle. It was the former home of Baron Walter von Richtofen, who established the suburb of Montclair in east Denver and promoted it as a resort and residential neighborhood. Aside from building his famous castle, Richtofen also built an art gallery, which once stood at the northwest corner of Eighth Avenue and Monaco Parkway, and a Molkeri, used when milk was thought to be a cure for tuberculosis. That building became city property in 1908 and has since been used for meetings, dances, parties, lectures, and a variety of educational classes. It is still extant at 6820 East Twelfth Avenue. Richtofen died practically bankrupt in 1898, and his widow moved to a quiet hotel to live out her days. Her ashes are interred in the fountain at the corner of Tenth Avenue and Oneida Street.

The thirty-room castle has been a Denver landmark for more than a century. When it was built in 1888 at 7020 East Twelfth Avenue, it was located far away from the center of town, and far away from practically anything else. It was one of the very first structures in that area and remained so for many years. Built of gray rusticated stone, it had the appearance of a medieval German castle. The rooms were large and impressive. The grounds were expansive, with many varieties of trees and bushes, and must have seemed like an oasis among the empty plain. Eventually, the grounds were enclosed with a tall stone wall, and a gatehouse was added to the east of the property.

When the Hendrie family moved in, a number of changes were made to the castle, and it was greatly enlarged. Its appearance was also altered to take on more of an English character. The entrance hall had walls of hand-tooled leather. The dining room was finished in oak, with leaded windows and French doors. The library boasted floor-to-ceiling bookshelves. Both the dining room and library opened onto their own sunporches. The expansive reception room, with a music corner built at one end, was finished in beech wood, and the fireplaces were of white marble.

Hendrie's daughter, Gertrude, married William W. Grant, Jr., nephew of Governor James B. Grant and son of Dr. William W. Grant, president of the Colorado State Medical Society. The couple raised their children in the castle, and after Edwin Hendrie died in 1932 at the age of eighty-five, the Grants remained in the house until 1936. The house has had a number of subsequent owners and was purchased twenty years ago by Gerald Priddy, owner of Estate Auctions. He and his wife, Esther, have filled the house with an array of appropriate antiques, acquired through their business and travels. They have recently placed the historic castle on the market.

The interior of the Richtofen castle.

Colorado Historical Society

Chapter 26

HERBERT COLLBRAN HOUSE

1277 WILLIAMS STREET

ARCHITECT: AARON GOVE

BUILT: CIRCA 1912

I n 1948, the sale of the Lester Friedman house at Thirteenth Avenue and Williams Street signaled the end of an era. At one time, Cheesman Park was almost entirely surrounded by mansions. Some still exist on the western edge of the park in the historic Humboldt Island District, including the Albert E. Humphreys house at 1022 Humboldt; the home of Harry H. Tammen, cofounder of the *Denver Post*, at 1061; and that of former Colorado Governor William Sweet, at 1075. A few survive on the eastern edge, most notably the former home of Henry Toll, at 919 Race Street, later owned by Fred Schmidt, barber turned successful merchandiser and appliance dealer. But most have been demolished over the years, to be replaced with high rise apartment buildings, especially on the east and north edges of the park.

The Collbran mansion was built as a gift from Adolph Coors, the brewery king, to his daughter, Augusta, who had married Herbert Collbran. The twenty-room house was modeled after the Petit Trianon at Versailles and was known as the city's first completely fireproof house. Its spacious rooms were furnished in contrasting European styles, each representing a historic period. The main floor consisted of a large drawing room, a music room, a sitting room, and a dining room, which was adjacent to the kitchen and pantry. The dining room, a former solarium, was especially impressive, with a polished marble floor, a colored glass ceiling copied from a Mexican cathedral, and a kneeling cherub looking over a marble fountain

The Herbert Collbran house, at the southwest corner of Thirteenth Avenue and Williams Street, was modeled after the Petit Trianon at Versailles.

and fish pond. The upstairs held six bedrooms, two baths, and a small parlor. Many of the furnishings and artwork were purchased in Europe during the Collbrans' travels.

Collbran had inherited his business acumen from his father, Henry, pioneer mining and railroad man. The senior Collbran was active in the development of railroads and the mining industry in Colorado, and in the overall development of the state. He was, at one time, president of the Colorado Midland Terminal Railway Company. Born in England in 1852, he moved to the United States in 1881, by that time having considerable experience in the rail and mining businesses. He also spent a great deal of time developing mines in Korea. He was a business partner with his son, Herbert, and with Adolph Coors, among others.

The house was sold only a few years after the Collbrans moved in to Leopold Guldman, founder of the Golden Eagle Department Store, a hugely successful enterprise located at Sixteenth and Lawrence streets in downtown Denver. Mr. Guldman was known for

his merchandising expertise and salesmanship, and his store was a mainstay for downtown shoppers for years. After Guldman's death, the house was purchased from Mrs. Guldman by her daughter, Mrs. Lester Friedman, who maintained residence there until she sold the property in 1948 to the Randell School, a college preparatory institution, that had previously held classes in the former John Perry home at 1280 Gilpin Street, now demolished. Randell School was founded in 1923 by Anna Randell and offered coeducational classes for 150 students from the first grade to the twelfth grade.

At the same time, another Cheesman Park mansion was being used for educational purposes. A former private mansion at 1275 High Street was opened in 1931 as the Peter Pan School. The name was changed in 1965 to the Cheesman Academy and at that time had 275 students. Run by Maude Miller, it gained a reputation as being one of the better scholastic institutions in the city, offering classes in art, art appreciation, piano, singing, dancing, French, and Spanish. Classes were from kindergarten to the sixth grade.

In 1970, a $7 million, twenty-four-story apartment building was planned with a connection to the academy. The income from the apartments was to help support classes there. This ambitious project was to have the high-rise building across the street from the school connected to the school via a bridge over High Street. Parents of the schoolchildren were to live in some of the apartments. While this concept never came to fruition, it was an advanced idea in Denver education that was never followed up.

The Randell School moved in the late 1960s to the former John Iliff estate in south Denver. The move brought about a firestorm of protest from residents around the Iliff property at 2160 South Cook Street. Miss Louise Iliff died at the age of ninety and willed the house and grounds to the Iliff School of Theology, which gave Randell School a thirty-day

option to buy the property. Charges were leveled that the Iliff School and the University of Denver, which also had holdings in the area, had violated deed restrictions that were to keep the area zoned R-1, or strictly residential.

Jack Wogan, a Denver developer, purchased the former Cheesman Academy property and offered the house to anyone who was willing to pay the cost of moving the structure. Another developer tried, but the cost was prohibitive, and the fact that the house was built mainly of sandstone made it an unstable proposition. Ultimately, the two mansions on Williams and Gilpin streets were torn down for the monolithic One Cheesman Place, one of many high-rise apartments to surround the park. The Collbran mansion is only vaguely remembered by older Denverites today.

The dining room of the Herbert Collbran house.

Denver Public Library Western History Collection

Chapter 27

LAWRENCE C. PHIPPS HOUSE

1156 EAST COLFAX AVENUE

ARCHITECT: THEODORE BOAL

BUILT: CIRCA 1886

Lawrence Cowle Phipps was one of the most remarkable men in Denver's history. He is unusual in that he didn't make his fortune in the state as most others did; he came to Colorado to retire after an extremely rewarding career in the steel industry back East. Born in Pennsylvania in 1862, he was schooled there and as a young man joined the firm of Carnegie Brothers & Company, where he progressed rapidly through the ranks. At the relatively young age of twenty-six, he was given a part interest in the business that made him a very wealthy man. A merger of the Frick coke companies, the Oliver mining interests, and the Carnegie interests formed the giant Carnegie Steel Corporation, and Phipps was elected its new vice-president. When he decided to take an early retirement and enjoy his earnings, he moved his family to Denver and rented the former William Bethel house at the corner of Colfax Avenue and Marion Street. The house was constructed in the early 1880s in the style of a Loire Valley chateau. Built of white boulder and white lava stone with a red-tile roof, the massive twenty-six-room mansion was filled with priceless antiques and artwork, including porcelain, paintings, and statuary.

Phipps eventually bought this mansion from Bethel in the early 1900s. Newspaper reporters used some flowery terms to describe the opening of the chateau by its new owners:

Ferril—Sketches of Colorado.

Lawrence C. Phipps.

The evening reception at which Mr. and Mrs. Lawrence Phipps were hosts last evening was far and away the handsomest and most elaborate social event which has been given in Denver this season. Society turned out en masse, and the elegant Phipps mansion at Colfax avenue and Marion street was formally thrown open for the first time for the reception of the guests. Although Mr. and Mrs. Phipps have been in their new home for more than a year, it has during that time been undergoing a thorough renovation and remodeling, and is now regarded without any exception as the handsomest residence in Denver. Last evening's affair was a sort of house warming and was the first entertaining that has been done in the new home. It was in the nature of a formal reception, lasting four hours. An elegantly appointed supper was served in the dining and breakfast rooms, which were elaborately and artistically decorated. The exquisite floral decorations blended harmoniously with the handsome frescoing and other interior adornment of

the house and was a most beautiful sight. The 100 guests, handsome in evening costume, presented a brilliant scene. Palms were profusely scattered about the house in every nook and corner, and each room was decorated in a style peculiar to itself with flowers of varied hue. Throughout the evening the orchestra furnished soft music from a balcony entwined with smilax and ferns. The receiving party stood before a bank of palms and American beauties. Altogether the affair was one not soon to be forgotten by Denver's society.

The house quickly became a center of Denver's social scene. The interior was decorated in the French Renaissance style, with heavy plasterwork on the walls and ceilings. A reception hall of twenty-five by twenty-five feet led to a number of main-floor rooms, including a library, a sitting room, a dining room, a breakfast room, a smoking room, a kitchen, and a long pantry. Most of these rooms were finished in oak or mahogany. Persian rugs and thick velvet carpets were spread on polished oak floors, and many of the walls were heavily paneled and frescoed. Bric-a-brac was everywhere throughout the house in high Victorian style, including Dresden figurines and vases, solid silver cups and urns, and cut-glass jars and bowls. A large marble copy of Canova's *Psyche* stood on a pedestal in the spacious drawing room. The ceiling of this room featured a hand-painted mural and decorative plasterwork. The Louis IV–style chairs and settees were covered in tapestries. Upstairs, a long hallway led to the many bedrooms, and a billiards room and shooting gallery were on the top floor, much to the amusement of Mr. Phipps's gentlemen friends. The house also had its own heating and ventilating plant.

Not one to remain idle for long, Phipps invested in numerous businesses and gave generously to the Children's Hospital, and the Denver Zoo. He financed Phipps Auditorium, which was built onto the east side of the Museum of Natural History at the east end of City Park. He donated funds for the Agnes Phipps Memorial Sanatorium in memory of his mother, who had died of tuberculosis (then known as the "white plague"). Colorado at that time was known for its clean air, and that disease had brought thousands to the state in a search for a cure. That building later served as the administration building for Lowry Air Force Base until it was demolished in 1963. Phipps also set up the Phipps Foundation. A Republican, he was elected to the U.S. Senate and served from 1919 to 1931. Throughout his life, he remained active in business and philanthropy.

When Phipps purchased the Bethel mansion, Colfax was one of three exclusive avenues in Capitol Hill, the other two being Grant Street and Sherman Street. His neighbor directly to the west was John W. Nesmith, one of the pioneers of Gilpin County. Nesmith was at one time the director of the Colorado Central Railroad, and he later became head of the Colorado Iron Works. In 1902, Nesmith sold his red-sandstone mansion to Jean Webb, president

of the Webb Pneumatic Cyanide Company, and he moved to the former Jeffrey Keating mansion at 1027 Pennsylvania Street. Catercorner to Nesmith's Colfax mansion was the Tuxedo Terrace, at 1101 East Colfax, built as a family-style apartment. It was three stories with steep steps to each of the four entrances. Built in the English tudor style of architecture, it catered to a well-heeled clientele and was one of the few terraces in the area that was tolerated by the neighboring home owners.

The early twentieth century brought commerce uptown and to Colfax, a relatively heavily traveled road. It was in proximity to many state buildings and seemed a likely prospect as a business street. Soon, small businesses of every sort, along with hotels and apartment buildings, were going up along the street, much to the consternation of the wealthy residents

The Captain William Bethel chateau at the southwest corner of Colfax and Marion, subsequently the home of Senator Lawrence Phipps, set the pace for later Colfax mansions.

Denver Public Library Western History Collection

The Lawrence Phipps mansion at 3400 Belcaro Drive.

who regarded Colfax as their exclusive territory. Many of the residents, including Senator Phipps, found the neighborhood less to their liking and moved out, some to the area east of Cheesman Park and some to the Denver Country Club area or beyond to the Polo Grounds. Phipps, who had been married twice previously, met and married Margaret Rogers. She was the daughter of Platt Rogers, a prominent Denver attorney who had a large house at the northeast corner of Colfax Avenue and Washington Street. The Phipps moved out of the Colfax Avenue chateau to a large house at 360 High Street in the Country Club area and soon began making plans to construct one of the city's showplace homes in south Denver, at 3400 Belcaro Drive.

Work began on the massive, thirty-two-room mansion. It was to become one of the largest construction projects in Colorado during the early years of the Great Depression. Hand-pressed bricks were carted to the ten-acre site by the truckload; stone was hand carved to specifications right on the property. The main entrance was flanked with stone Doric columns supporting a carved-stone cornice and an entablature with a broken pediment.

The grounds were laid out by landscapers according to Mrs. Phipps's plans, with large tiled patios in the rear of the house and stairs sloping gently down to the well-manicured lawn. The gardens were laid out with brick and stone walls containing recessed fountains and pierced brick parapets capped with Bedford stone coping and finials. A sunken garden included a spacious court surrounded by flagstone walkways.

When completed in 1932, the main house, built in a modified Georgian style, had fifteen rooms on the first floor, which included a large entrance hall, a living room, and a library. The dining room, with paneling in knotty pine and featuring hand-carved wood decorations over the fireplace, could seat forty guests. Mr. Phipps's office was also found on the main floor. The second floor contained nine bedrooms, baths, and dressing rooms, with servants' quarters on the top floor.

The house was filled with English period furnishings, with many antiques dating to the eighteenth century. A newspaper article carried the news of Mr. Phipps's purchase of two large tapestries that had formerly graced the walls of the royal palace in Stockholm. He was able to pick them up for $20,000 each, a bargain due to the worldwide Depression.

An interesting feature of the property was the immense tennis house that Mr. Phipps constructed for the amusement of his friends, and also as a way of keeping himself fit. Built in the English Tudor style, it boasted a lounge area, dressing rooms, loggias, a balcony, and a vast, arched ceiling. Slowly, other houses were built up around the mansion like so many satellites around the sun. The area became known as Belcaro.

Phipps lived in the mansion until his death in 1958 at the age of ninety-five. His widow gave up the house and moved to a smaller residence in the same area. The mansion was later given to the University of Denver for use as its conference center, and the house and tennis house are still extant. It was discreetly remodeled in a very sympathetic way, so as to keep the original integrity of the house while serving a new purpose as a part of the university. Phipps's son, Lawrence, Jr., became master of an estate south of Denver that was well publicized for the fact that it hosted the only fox hunts in the area. That property was to later become the core of the Highlands Ranch housing development.

Interior of the Phipps mansion.

Phipps Conference Center, University of Denver

Phipps Conference Center, University of Denver

The Phipps tennis house.

The East Colfax chateau was razed in the early 1930s, and for a time the property was the site of the Colfax Indoor Market, a large, enclosed shopping area that featured, among other things, a meat market, a fruit stand, a bakery, a coffee and spice company, a gift shop, a nut stand, a Safeway store, a potato-chip stand, a fish market, and a small restaurant. Built in the modern style of the 1930s, the building was white with large windows fronting Colfax and was topped with a wide, barrel roof. A large sign hung above the entrance, theater-style. There was also a two-pump filling station on the east side of the building. In the late 1950s, the Colfax Market closed and was demolished and replaced with the Heart of Denver Hotel, home to the Sword Room and the popular Tiki Lounge. The hotel is now operated as part of the Ramada chain. Phipps was married three times: to Isabella Loomis, who died in 1888; to Genevieve Chandler, whom he divorced in 1907, and Margaret Rogers, whom he married in 1911.

Chapter 28

Frederick G. Bonfils

1500 East Tenth Avenue

Architects: Aaron Gove & Thomas Walsh

Built: 1912

This forty-room behemoth, built on the western edge of Cheesman Park, was originally owned by Leo Guldman, founder of the Golden Eagle Department Store at Sixteenth and Lawrence streets. Because of his flashy advertising and promotions, he was considered one of the most successful merchandisers of his day. His store was, for many years, a mainstay of the downtown shopping district.

He later sold this house to Frederick G. Bonfils, flamboyant newspaperman, who, along with Harry H. Tammen, turned the *Denver Post* into a nationally recognized, if not highly criticized, newspaper. He and Tammen had purchased the struggling paper from a group of businessmen, including Charles J. Hughes, in 1895. Tammen had been in Denver for years, and Bonfils had migrated west from Missouri after running a number of businesses there. Tammen was somewhat quieter than Bonfils, a bit mischievous, and every bit the showman his partner was. He involved himself not only with the newspaper business, but also with his curio shop and his own circus, the Sells-Floto. The two very different personalities merged effectively to bring about the success of the *Post*. Throughout the early Bonfils/Tammen years, the *Post* was known as a sensationalistic operation, antagonistic toward many, and a finger-pointing scandal sheet bent on stirring up trouble, political and otherwise. In 1920, for example, the *Post* offices, then located between Fifteenth and Sixteenth streets on Champa Street, were stormed and practically destroyed by a mob of strikers during the violent Tramway strike, which the *Post*

Frederick G. Bonfils.

opposed in print. Another time, Bonfils was shot by an angry attorney as a result of the paper's crusade to parole cannibal Alferd Packer at the turn of the century. William "Buffalo Bill" Cody's funeral on Lookout Mountain, west of Denver, paid for by the *Post*, had an almost carnival-like atmosphere. And Bonfil's long-running feud with *Rocky Mountain News* owner Thomas Patterson was well publicized.

The partners devoted every waking hour to managing the paper, right up until Tammen's death in 1924. Thereafter, Bonfils ran the paper by himself. Aside from his interest in the newspaper, Bonfils had

Frederick G. Bonfils lived at 1003 Corona Street before moving to the southeast corner of Tenth Avenue and Humboldt Street.

Frederick Bonfils purchased this mansion at Tenth Avenue and Humboldt Street from department store owner Leopold Guldman.

acquired extensive holdings of common stocks, top-grade municipal and state bonds, and government bonds. He invested shrewdly in companies such as the Great Western Sugar Company, the Ideal Cement Company, the Denver Tramway Company, and the Denver Union Stockyards. He also invested wisely in oil and other natural resources. Downtown real estate also attracted his attention, and at the time of his death, large parcels of land passed down to his heirs. Bonfils could be considered one of the most influential people in early Colorado history.

The Bonfils home on East Tenth Avenue was a three-story house built in the neoclassical style on seven lots. It featured high ceilings, large rooms, and inlaid floors. It also boasted a swimming pool, and an auditorium in the basement. The extensive grounds, to the south, had gently sloping terraces, stairwells, and balustrades and included lush gardens with a large variety of flowers and trees. The separate three-car garage contained second-floor living quarters for the staff.

After Bonfils's death in 1933, his daughter Helen remained in the house until the late 1940s, when she sold it to the Conservative Baptist Theological Seminary. She moved to a large house at 707 Washington Street and continued her civic and social activities. An aspiring actress, she was heavily involved in local theater and donated land at Colfax Avenue and Elizabeth Street in the early 1950s for the construction of the Bonfils Theater, which she also financed. She also continued to involve herself with the running of the *Denver Post*, of which she became a major shareholder and later was elected chairwoman of the board.

After the seminary vacated the house on Tenth Avenue, it sat empty until it was razed in 1968 amid much protest, not only from preservation groups, but also from the neighbors of the Cheesman Park area who feared a proposed high-rise apartment building would interfere with their mountain view. After a few heated legal battles, the developers won out, and the high-rise went up as planned. This situation did much to heighten the awareness of the citizens of Denver regarding preservation and land use. A few of the original elements from the Bonfils house were incorporated into the new building, including some of the wrought-iron fencing that surrounded the property and two glass and iron light fixtures that graced either side of the mansion's entrance.

Chapter 29

HELEN BONFILS HOUSE

707 WASHINGTON STREET

ARCHITECT: MAURICE BISCOE

BUILT: 1908

The imposing white-stucco mansion at the corner of Seventh Avenue and Washington Street was built for Guilford Wood, who had been involved with J.S. Brown and the Brown Mercantile Company before branching out on his own in other, very profitable ventures. The house, designed in the Italian Renaissance style, was rich in detail and craftsmanship. The main floor contained the drawing room, a dining room, a library, and a kitchen. Four bedrooms were on the second level. After Wood's death, the house was sold to P. Randolph Morris, and the house was subsequently sold to Helen Bonfils when she gave up her father's palatial estate at Tenth Avenue and Humboldt Street to the Conservative Theological Seminary in 1948. Helen Bonfils was one of Denver's most influential citizens, as much so in her way as her father was in his. She promoted theater both locally and nationally and she gave her money generously to many worthy causes. Many benefited from the gifts she showered upon the city she loved.

She was born in New York in 1889 and came to Denver with her family at the time her father purchased the *Denver Post* in 1895. A trip as a young girl to the Tabor Grand Opera House inspired a lifelong love of the stage, and she and her childhood friends put on plays and musicals in the parlor of her family's mansion at 1003 Corona Street.

Colorado State Historical Society

Helen Bonfils (left) with then–Denver mayor Quigg Newton and singer Ethel Merman, circa 1950.

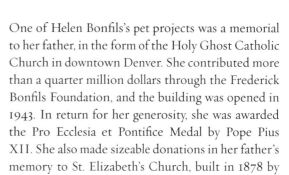

One of Helen Bonfils's pet projects was a memorial to her father, in the form of the Holy Ghost Catholic Church in downtown Denver. She contributed more than a quarter million dollars through the Frederick Bonfils Foundation, and the building was opened in 1943. In return for her generosity, she was awarded the Pro Ecclesia et Pontifice Medal by Pope Pius XII. She also made sizeable donations in her father's memory to St. Elizabeth's Church, built in 1878 by German immigrants and now part of the Auraria Campus.

Miss Bonfils was widowed in 1956, and three years later she married her driver, Edward "Tiger Mike" Davis, whom she had lavished gifts upon and set up in his own oil business. The marriage was not a healthy one, and rumors surfaced of arguments and physical violence. It was reported that she seemed meek in his presence, and as a staunch Catholic, she decided to suffer through it as best she could, rather than give up on her religious beliefs and face bitter divorce proceedings that were bound to cost her a great deal of money. Her health began to decline, and some thought that she didn't seem as mentally sharp as she once had been. They later divorced.

As Miss Bonfils became more unstable, rumors flared that perhaps she was being taken advantage of by some of those close to her. She had many visitors to her private suite of rooms at St. Joseph Hospital, both official and unofficial.

She died on June 6, 1972 at the age of eighty-two. Information was published in the *Rocky Mountain News* two months later alleging that the late newspaper heiress had signed away to a trust a personal fortune of more than $8 million. That was the amount at stake when eleven relatives contested the will, charging that Miss Bonfils was mentally unfit when she made her last will. They pointed out that two houses had been deeded to her former husband, Edward "Tiger Mike" Davis, which were included in the terms of her divorce settlement. They were the house at 707 Washington Street and another mansion that sat at 700 Pearl Street, directly west. A month after her death, "Tiger Mike" received $1 million from Edward Doumani, in whose favor Davis executed a deed of trust on the two properties. Helen Bonfils left assets

Miss Bonfils attended the exclusive Wolcott School for Girls, at East Fourteenth Avenue and Marion Street, which is now an apartment building. She continued her acting and gained experience in student productions in college. Early in her career, she took on roles at Denver's Elitch Theater and soon became a member of the stock company. Here she met George Somnes, the theater's director, and they were married in 1936. Their marriage received widespread publicity, and it was reported that she was one of the wealthiest women in the West. She embarked on a successful career as a producer in New York and was also involved in the Denver Civic Theater, whose plays were then held at the University of Denver Theater. She also sponsored the annual Cheesman Park operas, free to the public and given from a specially built stage at the park pavilion.

In the early 1940s, Miss Bonfils purchased lots at the southwest corner of Colfax Avenue and Elizabeth Street with the idea of building a new civic theater where she and her husband could showcase new plays and new local actors. It wasn't until the early 1950s, however, that plans came to fruition and the Bonfils Theater opened to an appreciative audience. Over the next few decades, many first-rate productions were held there, and the theater gained national prominence.

Helen Bonfils and her sister May were extremely competitive and did not always get along well. Theirs was a continuous test of one-upsmanship.

The Helen Bonfils mansion at Seventh Avenue and Washington Street was later remodeled into condos.

of only $263,819. According to a *News* article dated July 30 of that same year, "that was only a fraction of the total assets that were in her command before she signed her will last Oct. 12. On that same day a second document was brought to her, by which she signed away at least $5.4 million in personal assets to a trust which is under the control of two *Denver Post* executives who now refuse to comment on its purpose, its beneficiaries, its total worth, or their personal stake in administering it." Her very complicated estate made it nearly impossible to straighten out. Accusations abounded along with charges of double dealing among some of her former business associates. As a result, her estate was not settled for well over a decade.

The Sheedy mansion at Eleventh Avenue and Grant Street, which served for so many years as fine-arts studios, was sold, and the long-time tenants were given notice to vacate the premises. Most of them had been touched by Miss Bonfils's generosity in

the fact that she charged nominal rents, sometimes far below the going rates, and helped to financially support many of them, quietly and without public acknowledgment.

The Washington Street mansion was purchased by a group of investors, including former Colorado Lieutenant Governor Mark Hogan, in the early 1980s. The house was divided into three apartments. Two buildings to the west were torn down for construction of twenty-three townhomes, built in the same style as the main house and forming a complex of luxury units.

Chapter 30

MAY BONFILS STANTON HOUSE

WADSWORTH BOULEVARD &
WEST ALAMEDA AVENUE

ARCHITECT: J.J. (JACQUES) BENEDICT

BUILT: CIRCA 1930

May Bonfils came to Denver in the mid-1890s at the time her father, Frederick G. Bonfils, bought the *Denver Post* from Charles Hughes and others. She and her sister, Helen, led privileged lives and were doted on by both parents. She attended the exclusive Wolcott School for Girls, located at Fourteenth Avenue and Marion Street, now used as an apartment complex, and St. Mary's Academy when that institution was located downtown. She graduated from Brownell Hall in New York and soon after went abroad on an extended trip with her father. While in Europe, she studied singing and piano, dance, languages, art, and etiquette—all the requisites for a society lady of the day.

In 1904, she wed Clyde Berryman. They were divorced in 1946 after a long separation. She remarried in 1957, this time to Charles Edwin Stanton, a Denver architect and interior designer. From the time of her divorce until her second marriage, she was a virtual recluse at her grand estate in west Denver. Her second husband encouraged her to resume an active life, and she became interested in civic works. She donated large amounts of money in her later years, most notably to Loretto Heights College and for the decoration of the Catholic Chapel at the Air Force Academy at Colorado Springs. She met Charles Stanton while he was redecorating the Teller House in Central City, and she became interested in the area. She gave funds for care of the garden that connects the Teller House with the Central City Opera House.

Exterior of the May Bonfils Stanton estate.

In the mid-1930s, she hired architect Jacques Benedict to design a flamboyant copy of the Petit Trianon, the retreat built by Louis XVI for his mistress, Marie Antoinette. The 250-acre site that she chose was, at that time, far out in the country and was part of a private game preserve owned by her father. The house was situated in open space and had a commanding view of a private lake and the Rocky Mountains in the distance. The twenty-room mansion was built of white Cararra marble, with hand-wrought iron balustrades, cut-glass windows, and acres of well-manicured lawns and gardens. The drive to the main entrance was flanked with

fruit trees and marble statuary. The centerpiece of the entrance was a marble fountain with a statue of Venus by the famous sculptor Canova. The Stantons entertained frequently in a lavish style, although the dinners included no more than a few close friends and associates. The house was filled with artwork purchased during her occasional trips to Europe, and it was constructed to display her important collection to its best advantage.

The library became the central showcase for much of this art, and it was filled with sculptures of marble and bronze. Some were original, and some were

There was also a menagerie of deer, sheep, and swans at the estate. Occasionally, visitors to the house would notice the Napoleon crest displayed discreetly throughout the place, in reference to Frederick Bonfils's ancestral ties to the Little Corporal.

Mrs. Stanton became known locally as "the last of the Victorians," due to the fact that she frequently refused to acknowledge the twentieth century. Her clothes were made exclusively for her by the famed Fontana House in Rome. Her perfumes came directly from Paris. Her jeweler, one of New York's most prominent, often flew to Denver to show Mrs. Stanton some of his newest acquisitions. The bedroom where she spent her last days was filled with bronzes, carved ivory, a fainting couch, hand-painted fans, French porcelains, and other items, surrounding a bed reputedly owned by Marie Antoinette.

May Bonfils Stanton died in March 1962, survived by her husband and her sister.

The house was sold soon after, and the furniture and other treasures were auctioned off. Her fabled jewelry collection, valued at more than $2 million, was sold at auction in New York. Her collection included some of the largest diamonds and sapphires in the region.

The house was donated by Mr. Stanton to the Denver Catholic Archdiocese. It was subsequently demolished to make way for the Villa Italia Shopping Center and an adjacent housing development. The property was also used for the new Lakewood Municipal Government Center, the Lakewood Heritage Center, and Belmar Park.

The fountain that graced the grounds, also designed by Benedict, was moved to the Hungarian Freedom Park, at Clarkson Street and Speer Boulevard.

replicas, but many were displayed on a giant table and cabinet from the Versailles Palace made by the famous cabinetmaker, Charles Boulle. The paintings displayed on the library walls included a Correggio, a Corot, and a Van Dyck.

The drawing room of the house featured walls of pink damask silk bordered in gold frames and was furnished with items from some of the great houses of England, such as Holyrood and St. James Palace. A chair that May Stanton used to hold court once belonged to Queen Victoria and bore the royal crest. A marble copy of Canova's *The Three Graces* faced the sloping terrace, where there was a large reflecting pool. Beyond was Belmar Lake.

MRS. VERNER Z. REED HOUSE

475 CIRCLE DRIVE

ARCHITECT: HARRY MANNING

BUILT: 1929–30

There were some who were rich enough to weather the storm of the Great Depression comfortably, and one such person was Mrs. Verner Z. Reed, widow of one of Colorado's most important and enterprising pioneers. Verner Z. Reed was one of Colorado's wealthiest citizens, having invested in the oil industry; numerous gold, silver, and copper mines; and large parcels of real estate. Born in Ohio in 1863, he moved at an early age to Iowa, where he attended school. As a young man, he left for Chicago to join the staff of the *Chicago Tribune* as a journalist, but he was sidetracked by the lure of gold discoveries in the West. He soon came to Colorado. By this time, he had met and married Mary Dean Johnson, and they settled in the Colorado Springs area, where he began investing in real estate.

When the Cripple Creek area was being developed, Verner Reed was one of the first to involve himself with local business interests. He had earned a $1 million commission in 1901 for selling Winfield Stratton's Independence Mine to an English syndicate, and his fortune grew from this broad foundation. He invested in the Western Sugar Land Company and was an early developer of the Cripple Creek area. After earning his commission he and his wife sailed for Europe, where they lived for more than a decade in Paris, Rome, and the south of France.

They returned to the United States in 1913, and Reed continued to expand his fortune with the accumulation of oil fields in Wyo-

The Mrs. Verner Z. Reed residence.

ming. The Reeds had purchased the former Stoiber residence at 1022 Humboldt Street, where they entertained lavishly. Among their guests was John D. Rockefeller, Jr. An article from the *Denver Post* of September 29, 1915, gives a glowing description of the event:

> One of the last guests to leave the elaborately appointed dinner dance at the Verner Z. Reeds was John D. Rockefeller Jr., who basked in the smiles of the charming honor guest, Miss Cynthia Edrington, and whiled away the evening dancing and dividing his attentions among the attractive women present. The party decorations were exceptionally handsome and indeed a tribute to the florist's art, for the choicest of fall colorings were combined to give a wondrous effect thruout the spacious rooms. Later in the afternoon each of the women and young girls who were included on the guest list received a beautiful corsage of orchids and lilies, sent by the host, and upon arrival each gentleman found at his dinner placement a little boutonniere of tiny French rosebuds. Following the magnificent dinner and hours of dancing to the small orchestra, in fact shortly after midnight a sumptuous supper was served and the guests who lingered until nigh on 3 o'clock a.m. were loathe to take their departure even at that early morning hour. Among the almost one hundred guests were Mr. and Mrs. Crawford Hill, Courtland Dines, Grover Coors, Ira Humphreys, F.G. Bonfils, Lawrence Phipps, Helen Bonfils, Henry Van Schaack, George Gano and Jesse Welborn.

The couple also traveled extensively, mostly to Europe, where they pursued their interests in art and history, sometimes purchasing antiques and artwork to be shipped back to Denver.

Verner Z. Reed died in 1919 and was interred in the family mausoleum at Mount Olivet Cemetery. Mrs. Reed became increasingly involved in the charitable dispersal of her husband's fortune, donating large amounts of money to Denver University, and she was responsible for the construction of the Margery Reed Hall, in memory of her daughter, who

had died at a young age in 1925. She also donated money for the design and construction of the Mary Reed Library on the campus. Mrs. Reed was named to the board of trustees of the university in 1929. She founded the Margery Reed Mayo Children's Nursery at 1128 Twenty-Eighth Street and contributed to other causes as well. She paid for construction of the girls' dormitory at the University of Colorado and helped to support Colorado General Hospital and the Colorado School of Mines in Golden. The Reeds also had two sons, Verner, Jr. and Joseph. Verner, Jr. built a home in west Denver that later became the Green Gables Country Club. He moved from Denver to Newport, Rhode Island. Joseph made his home in New York.

Mrs. Reed owned a number of properties, among them a large parcel of land just south of Sixth Avenue and west of University Boulevard in what was then known as Park Lane Square. When she decided to sell the house on Humboldt Street, she commissioned Harry Manning to design a large, Tudor-style residence at 475 Circle Drive. The palatial home was built of crème-colored brick and accented in Indiana limestone. It exhibits heavy Jacobean influence.

Italian marble was used for the fireplaces and the flooring. Everything in the house was custom-made. The outer doors were of bronze and wrought iron. The main level consisted of a large drawing room, a library, a kitchen, a large dining room, a central hallway with a winding staircase and creme travertine flooring, a sunroom, and suite of guest rooms. The second level contained four bedrooms, two of which had their own outside terraces. A retinue of gardeners kept the expansive grounds, including a variety of trees, bushes, and flowers, in manicured condition. Also on the property is a fountain of marble and bronze and a large, naturalized reflecting pond.

When Mrs. Reed died in 1945, the inheritance tax on her estate was the largest on record in Colorado up to that time. The house was sold through her heirs the following year to Joseph Minnisale, Denver real estate executive and head of Minnisale Realty Company. The Minnisales were known for their outstanding parties, and they entertained on a lavish scale. They lived in the house until 1977, when it was sold to Fred Ebrahimi, who had varied business interests, including Quark, the software company, which he financed along with Tim Gill.

Detail of the Reed mansion.

Author's Collection

Chapter 32

William Church House

1000 Corona Street

Architects: William Lang
& Marshall Pugh

Built: circa 1890

After William Church made his fortune in mining and cattle, he commissioned architects William Lang and Marshall Pugh to design this Romanesque Revival castle for himself and his family. The house cost $40,000, a phenomenal amount of money at the time. The stables cost an additional $4,500. In 1890, an eight-room furnished house would rent for fifteen dollars a month, and a seven-room house would sell for $3,500.

Church came to Colorado from Illinois in 1866, at the age of twenty-five. He immediately became involved in mining in Clear Creek, Gilpin, and Boulder counties. In 1880, he went to Arizona, where he developed copper-mining interests. After returning to Denver, he began investing in real estate. He also owned a large ranch near Silver City, New Mexico, where he raised cattle. Other business interests included the manufacture of bricks and soap.

This twenty-five-room castle, built of gray rusticated stone, featured a reception hall that was heavily paneled with hardwoods. A staircase with a removable railing doubled as a stage for the many musicales that were held in the mansion. The library boasted stained-glass windows, hand-tooled leather covering the upper walls, and carved paneling in Moorish design, with a Persian-style fireplace. The whole of the main floor was exotic in design and was finished in many different hardwoods.

Prominent Denver architects Land & Pugh designed this castle for mining tycoon William Church.

The house also boasted a two-manual pipe organ. The pipes ran underneath the stage landing. A room adjacent to the stage could be thrown open to accommodate extra guests. The spacious drawing room featured a large, cut-glass window imported from Paris that cast rainbows across the room. A photographic darkroom and a bowling alley were located in the basement. The tower held the servants' quarters.

After Church's unexpected death in 1901, his heirs sold the property and left the state. By the early 1920s, it was being operated as the Castle Hotel. A newspaper advertisement of the day touted "nice, large rooms, private baths, special rates for 2. 1 single room with running water, excellent home-cooked meals. $7 per week, garage $5." The name was later changed to the Tutwiler, and it was operated as a rooming house. In the 1930s, it was rumored that a group of drug smugglers was operating out of the house. During the Second World War, it was used as housing for soldiers' families, and in 1945, it was again a rooming house, this time called the Southland Guest House. It changed names again in the late 1950s and remained a guest home until it was finally closed up and wrecked in 1965. The land was used for the construction of two apartment buildings separated by a parking lot.

Interior of the William Church residence.

HORACE TABOR HOUSE

1260 SHERMAN STREET

ARCHITECT: UNKNOWN

BUILT: 1878

The Tabor saga is well known throughout Colorado and the West. Horace A.W. Tabor, after years of plodding along in the mining camps of Colorado, struck it rich through his investments in the Little Pittsburgh and Matchless mines, among others. Money poured in at an incredible rate and made Tabor a millionaire many times over. A master at self-promotion, Tabor's name was soon recognized by everyone in town as he spent his money lavishly, first building the Tabor Opera House there and donating to various causes around the town. He was a promoter of the Leadville water system and was one of the incorporators of the Leadville Gas Company. He was elected town mayor and served from 1878-1879. It wasn't long before he yearned for bigger things, and he soon moved his quiet and dignified wife, Augusta, to Denver.

Tabor, who was a force to be reckoned with, took the city by storm, flashing diamond stick pins and swinging gold-tipped walking canes. With his steady flow of cash, he immediately began erecting stone monuments to himself and his name; the Tabor Block, at Sixteenth and Larimer streets, and the Tabor Grand Opera House, were but two of the many monoliths bearing his name. The Tabor Grand opened to an awestruck public. It was something the people of Denver had never seen, and for years it was unsurpassed as the region's fantasy world of entertainment. The huge interior was decorated with exotic woods, heavy velvet draperies, and murals and paintings by local artists. The multi-storied building was a sight to

Ferril—Sketches of Colorado.

Horace A.W. Tabor.

behold to many who traveled from dusty little burgs to witness in person what had been related to them by friends and relatives.

Tabor was generous to his own friends and relatives and employed many of them, and even some of Augusta's kin who had moved West from Maine, her birthplace. The Denver directory of 1890 lists no less than three Tabors—George, Jonathan, and Lemuel—working in different capacities in either the Tabor Opera House or in the Tabor Block. The Tabors' son, N. Maxcy, started his successful business career working for his father.

Before the Capitol Hill neighborhood was settled, one of the first landmark houses in the area was built on what was then the edge of the city, at Seventeenth Avenue and Broadway. The house was built in 1874 for Henry Cordes Brown, Denver capitalist and real-estate speculator, and was considered to be one of the costliest and handsomest residences in all of Denver.

Brown came to Denver by ox team in 1860, at the age of forty. He had already been engaged in the

lumber business in Washington state and then set about traveling the world in search of his fortune. His travels took him to California, Peru, Missouri, and Nebraska. Once he arrived in Denver, he took up the carpentry trade. He had staked a preemption claim to a tract of land that later became known as "Brown's Bluff." This ten-acre plot included much of what was to become Capitol Hill and Quality Hill. The State Capitol Building was erected on a site that was owned by Brown and donated to the city. Brown continued to buy up land for speculation and became wealthy in the process. The nine-story sandstone and granite Brown Palace Hotel, which he built, was opened in 1892 on land that was part of this tract. Directly east of the hotel was where he decided to build his mansion. Brown lived in the house for a few years before selling it to Horace Tabor, who purchased it for his wife, Augusta. Brown then settled in a fashionable house at the northwest corner of Thirteenth Avenue and Sherman Street.

Mrs. Tabor, whose tastes were more pedestrian than those of her husband, rejected the extravagance of the Broadway house and was highly displeased with her husband's ever-increasing lust for money and celebrity. She had, through all the trials and tribulations of a dutiful Victorian wife, stuck by his side during the roughest of times, while his search for fortune took them to rugged and dangerous places. While living in the mining camps, the Tabors regularly took in boarders for extra income. They also, however, gave help to those in need, offering shelter and food either free of charge or on credit. They were respected as kind, generous, hard-working people and were generally well liked. Mrs. Tabor more or less followed the same pattern in the Broadway house, giving shelter to acquaintances and relatives alike the entire time she lived there.

The house sat on property that took up most of the block bounded by Broadway, Lincoln, and Seventeenth and Eighteenth avenues. The original address was listed alternately as 96 Broadway (before the renumbering of Denver's streets in the early 1900s) and 1733 Lincoln Street. It was built three stories high of red brick with white wood trim. The rooms were spacious, with high ceilings and large windows. The entire house was furnished in the elaborate Victorian

The Horace Tabor house at Seventeenth Avenue and Broadway later became the Commercial Club before being torn down to make way for progress.

style of the day. The grounds, which sloped gently from Lincoln down to Broadway, were immaculately maintained by a crew of gardeners, who planted a variety of trees, bushes, and flowering shrubs.

The house quickly became the social center of the region, and many of the Tabors' relatives, friends, and business associates were regularly invited. A glowing write-up in the *Rocky Mountain News* of January 1881 gave this account:

> The reception at the Tabor residence on New Year's, which escaped the attention of the press at the time, was one of the most splendid events of the day, and has called out more than usual comment and admiration. The beautiful and commodious rooms were decorated in the most gorgeous style, wherein good taste formed a conspicuous part, and the attendance of ladies assisting was such a selection as the gods might have

made. Mrs. Tabor was attired in cream embossed satin, point lace and diamond ornaments, together with fresh cardinal flowers. Mrs. Trimble in black silk and velvet and a great profusion of diamonds. Miss Hughes was dressed in green watered silk and velvet, with Valenciennes lace and diamonds. Miss McFerran was attired in French blue silk, trimmed with gold brocade and diamonds.

> The tables, which were well patronized, were elaborately decorated with fresh cut flowers and fruit, and all the delicacies of the season were served by the attentive and well-trained waiters. Over 250 gentlemen left cards.

Although the parties given at the Tabor house were generally for the well-heeled and upper crust of Denver society at the time, this was probably in consideration of Horace's business connections and political aspirations, and not of Augusta's personal preferences. She was not impressed with the show of wealth that now surrounded her and was quite content to spend her time with her relatives and people she knew from her earlier days in Maine and Leadville. But she was a dutiful wife and gave in to the demands expected of her, as she had done throughout her marriage.

While Horace busied himself with his varied interests, Augusta maintained the house and was involved with local social and civic causes. Devoutly religious, she was a member of, and gave money to, the Unitarian Unity church, on Nineteenth Avenue and Broadway, and gave of her time and money to the Ladies' Aid Society, of which she was elected vice-president.

As time wore on, the Tabors' marriage wore thin, and the strain became evident to those close to the couple. Horace's disdain for his wife's temperament and his desire for a livelier and more sympathetic companion led him to look elsewhere. There were already rumors of Tabor's infidelity, rumors that couldn't be proven but that were hurtful to Augusta just the same. By now, Horace had met and become romantically involved with Elizabeth "Baby Doe" McCourt, a gorgeous and impetuous woman who was previously married to Harvey Doe. It wasn't long before Horace had set up Baby Doe in lavish style in a suite of rooms at the fashionable Windsor Hotel on Eighteenth Street and Larimer. Rumors were soon running rampant, and Horace moved out of the Broadway house for good and into the Windsor to join his lover. In 1883, the Tabors were divorced, under great protest from Augusta, and Horace was soon married to Baby Doe in a lavish ceremony in Washington, D.C., attended by, among others, President Chester Arthur.

Mrs. Tabor was awarded the house along with numerous other properties in her divorce settlement from her husband, and she became one of the wealthiest women in the West. She continued her involvement in various charities and civic works, but life without Horace would never be the same. She moved out of the Broadway house and into the

Brown Palace Hotel across the street. In the mid-1890s, she became ill and, hoping for a recovery, moved temporarily to Pasadena, California, where she took a suite of rooms in a hotel. Her condition worsened, and she died in February 1895. She is buried in Riverside Cemetery in north Denver.

In 1894, the Commercial Club took a long lease on the Broadway property, together with the half-block of garden surrounding it. The house was overhauled on the interior to meet the needs of the club, which was formed two years earlier and was one of the leading social organizations of Denver. Its members numbered around 250 and included some of the city's most prominent businessmen. Its previous quarters had been downtown on Arapahoe Street. The club also made plans to build an addition, forty-five by sixty feet, to accommodate the billiard room and other recreation areas. The grounds were also replanted with a variety of flowering trees and flower beds.

Less than ten years later, in June 1903, crews moved onto the property to begin the process of tearing down the mansion to make way for a number of commercial structures on the block. The new owners wanted to take advantage of the fact that commercial enterprise was rapidly surrounding the mansion and the property was ripe for development. The Metropole Hotel and storefronts facing Broadway had already been built, edging ominously close to the old Tabor place, and would later be joined by the Cosmopolitan Hotel at Eighteenth Avenue and Broadway. The first load of earth had been turned when the plow struck a relic of thirty years earlier, a broken terra-cotta piece that was once an ornament on a large fountain that was the centerpiece of the driveway to the house. It had been buried under a mound of dirt and forgotten.

Baby Doe was more than happy to settle into a life of luxury, and she complimented Tabor's exuberance in public. As the Broadway mansion was given to his former wife in the divorce, Tabor, tiring of living at the Windsor, began looking around for permanent quarters for himself and Baby Doe. He found such a place, originally built by Joseph Bailey in 1878, at 1260 Sherman Street. The house featured spacious

The Sherman Street interior shows the much-loved excess in Victorian decorating. The picture on the left is of Lillie Tabor, daughter of Horace and Baby Doe.

rooms, carved woodwork throughout the house, and black slate fireplaces. Tabor filled the rooms with expensive furniture and bric-a-brac. The sprawling grounds covered most of the block bounded by Thirteenth Avenue, Twelfth Avenue, Grant Street, and Sherman Street. The Tabors filled the yard with iron deer and fountains made of copper and lead. The large stables held at least three carriages, complete with coachman and footman.

Horace and Baby Doe, the subject of much gossip and newspaper space, were a notorious couple and were talked about, in hushed tones, wherever they went. They were written up in newspaper articles and always created a stir whenever they were spotted in public, either individually or together. To the people of nineteenth-century Denver, they represented the end result of drive, ambition, and good fortune.

But eventually their luck ran out. Tabor started losing money—a lot of money. He had made bad investments, given out bad loans, generally overspent,

and lost a great deal in the Silver Panic of 1893. Before long, he was so short of cash that the water and gas were turned off in the mansion. The Tabors were forced to move out, and they occupied several small houses while trying to scrape by.

Horace took a room in a downtown hotel and soon sent for his wife and two daughters, Silver Dollar and Lillie. His luck was starting to take a turn for the better when he was made Denver's postmaster, but he died unexpectedly in 1899, leaving Baby Doe penniless. She eventually moved back to Leadville, to a small shack at the Matchless Mine, one of the mines that had given the Tabors so much wealth. She survived there mainly with the help of friends and her brother, Peter McCourt, who was a successful theater manager in Denver. She spent a great deal of time, and took many trips to Denver, trying to interest investors in opening the Matchless one more time, to no avail. Over the following years she aged, and her great beauty faded. Her trips to Denver became infrequent, and she presented quite a sight to passersby when she was spotted walking downtown in moth-eaten clothes, dirty boots, and a disheveled hat. Now she was left with only the memories of what once had been.

In 1935, Baby Doe was found frozen to the floor of her shack, bringing to an end one of the most colorful and romantic stories in Colorado history.

The Sherman Street mansion was next occupied by George Tritch, local businessman, who held on to it for a few years. In 1919, the house was wrecked to make way for a proposed state armory building.

The plan apparently never came to fruition, as the site remained vacant for many years afterward. The block was eventually built up with new houses and apartments and some commercial structures. The last holdouts were the Charles Boettcher mansion, at 1201 Grant Street, torn down in 1953, and the William Fullerton mansion, just to the west on Sherman Street, torn down at the same time to make way for the Colorado Department of Employment Building. The Tabor property is now occupied by a 1950s apartment building.

Tabor bought the Joseph Bailey mansion at 1260 Sherman Street for Baby Doe, his wife and former mistress.

Denver Public Library Western History Collection

Chapter 34

ERASTUS HALLACK HOUSE

1701 SHERMAN STREET

ARCHITECT: UNKNOWN

BUILT: CIRCA 1890

One of the most important figures in the development of the city and state was Erastus F. Hallack, who built up the fledgling lumber industry to major prominence in the last quarter of the nineteenth century. As a principal owner of the Hallack-Howard Lumber Company, then the Hallack-Sayre-Newton Lumber Company, and the Hallack Paint and Oil Company, he supplied much-needed materials to an ever-expanding city.

Hallack was born in 1830 in New York. His father was a farmer, an occupation in which Hallack had little interest. He set his sights toward more adventurous activities and soon left home to pursue his ambitions. He first moved to Illinois, where he became involved in the building of horse carriages. It wasn't long before he moved to Kansas and became a stock trader. In the early 1860s, he bought some ox teams and established a freight business between the Missouri River and Denver, hauling mainly corn but also some goods and supplies, making his money on commission.

With his proceeds, he invested in a lumber company, along with a partner, J.H. Morrison—a partnership that lasted five years. Morrison retired and Hallack became partners with his brother Charles. Together they formed the Hallack Brothers Lumber Company. The venture took off and became successful and widely known. The two brothers also became involved in banking and real estate. Erastus Hallack was one of the founders of the Rocky Mountain

Colorado State Historical Society

Built to showcase Hallack's lumber business, all the rooms of his residence featured elaborately carved wood moulding, paneling, and other decorations.

The interior of the Hallack residence at 1701 Sherman Street shortly before its destruction in 1941.

Construction Company, which later merged with the Denver Union Water Company, operated by Walter Cheesman and a number of other city leaders.

Secure in his career, Hallack built a home for himself and his wife, Kate, at the northeast corner of Nineteenth Avenue and Lincoln Street, which then was considered to be in the country. By the standards of the times, it was quite a showplace. It was one of the first homes in the city to have a winding staircase, and it boasted two fountains in the front yard, much to the delight of dusty passersby. The Hallacks had an unobstructed view of the entire front range. This oasis in the middle of a dry plain must have been a sight to behold.

As Hallack's career gained momentum, he sold the house to General William Palmer, who helped bring the railroads to Colorado and later was instrumental in the founding of Colorado Springs. Hallack built a larger home at Nineteenth Avenue and Sherman Street, and it soon became a center of social activity in the city.

As the Hallacks' social ambitions expanded, the need for a larger and more fashionable house became evident, and they built it on a grand scale at 1701 Sherman Street. There they entertained lavishly; the house was graced by most of the important people of the city. By that time, Hallack had become a powerful influence in the city. Although he held no public office, he was nominated time and time again—once for governor—all of which he politely turned down. Mrs. Hallack was a doyenne of early Denver society. She became a member of the Colorado Chapter of the Daughters of the American Revolution and founded the General Federation of Women's Clubs.

The house was typical of the unrestrained exuberance of the era, when vast amounts of money were made quickly and there were no income taxes. No expense was spared in the construction of the home, from carefully chosen woods for the interior, much of it hand carved, to the imported cut-glass and stained-glass windows. The hardware, such as locks and hinges, throughout the house were of brass or bronze. Specially made fixtures lighted the rooms. Attention was given to every detail of design, and nothing was overlooked. Much of the construction was overseen by Mrs. Hallack.

The imposing house, built in the Queen Anne style, sat on spacious grounds with stables in the back of the property. Just west of the Hallack place was the former home of David Moffat, at 1706 Lincoln Street, where he lived before building his monolith at 808 Grant Street.

Erastus died in 1897, and Kate Hallack continued to live in the mansion with a small staff. By the time she died, at the age of ninety-one in 1938, she shared her neighborhood with apartments, shops, auto garages, and other commercial structures. The homes of her neighbors had long since been torn down or turned into boardinghouses. The Hallack house was sold by her estate and wrecked in 1941, and the property remained vacant for years. Eventually, the Hallack and Moffat land was swallowed up by the multistory United Bank Building, which stretches from Lincoln to Sherman streets along Seventeenth Avenue.

35

JULIUS MYERS HOUSE

1205 OGDEN STREET

ARCHITECT: UNKNOWN

BUILT: CIRCA 1892

A low sandstone retaining wall is all that remains of a house almost completely forgotten, even by longtime Denverites. A red brick mansion was erected in the early 1890s at 1205 Ogden Street for H.B. Chamberlain. It had the standard Victorian accouterments, such as leaded-windows, brass lighting fixtures, brass doorknobs and door hinges, carved woodwork throughout the house, and prominent dormers and bay windows, all fronted by a large wooden veranda. Chamberlain did not own the property for long, and it was sold in 1894 to Mr. and Mrs. Julius A. Myers. They had previously lived at Twenty-Eighth and Champa streets.

Myers was born in Ohio in 1848, and as a young man he enlisted in the service. After the end of the Civil War, he came to Colorado and immediately became involved in the state's fledgling railroad business. He rose through the ranks to become superintendent of the Denver & Rio Grande at Salida, having started out as a telegrapher. He also served as paymaster of the Union Pacific at Cheyenne. It was during this time that he met and married Hattie Eaton, and the couple had one daughter, Mabel, who would become one of the city's noted society girls, known for her beauty and charm. The family suffered a bitter blow when she died at an early age in 1911, shortly after her marriage, leaving the Myers to bear their overwhelming grief together. Every day they visited the mausoleum they had built for their daughter in Fairmont Cemetery, putting fresh flowers on her grave.

The Julius Myers residence at 1205 Ogden Street.

Myers was well known for his business savvy and was one of the original owners of the Salt Creek oil fields in Wyoming. He formed a partnership with Horace Bennett, another prominent businessman. It became a bond that was to be mutually beneficial, both financially and socially. The firm of Bennett and Myers became synonymous with some of the most important real-estate deals of the 1880s and 1890s. In partnership with others, they were responsible for the construction of the Empire, Majestic, and Enterprise buildings and the modernization of the Tabor Grand Opera House Block, which they took over in 1908.

The pair purchased tracts of ranch land west of Colorado Springs. The town of Cripple Creek was surveyed on one of the tracts in 1891, and more than one-half million dollars worth of lots were sold when gold was discovered, creating a demand for housing and other buildings. Ever civic-minded, Myers served as a member of the city council and was partly responsible for the city's purchase of a large tract of land that would become City Park.

The Ogden Street house was spacious and had heavy, carved woodwork throughout. A large entryway featured a fireplace with a carved mantle. Among the rooms found on the main floor were the drawing room, complete with fireplace and heavy ceiling beams, a dining room, a music room, and a library. A large kitchen and a butler's pantry were located on this floor. The house was large enough to accommodate 500 people during one of Mrs. Myers' parties.

After Myers' death in 1918, his widow sold the house. It remained in private hands for a few decades, after which it became the Ogden Hotel, and later a rooming house. It then fell into a state of decay. It was vacant for a few years. Windows were broken, woodwork was damaged, and the house generally was vandalized. It was rumored by local schoolchildren to be haunted. The Myers mansion was torn down unceremoniously in the mid-1960s to make way for a modern apartment building.

Chapter 36

THOMAS CROKE/ THOMAS PATTERSON HOUSE

428 EAST ELEVENTH AVENUE

ARCHITECT: ISAAC HODGSON

BUILT: 1891

This house, built for Thomas Croke in the style of a Loire Valley chateau, has been a Denver landmark for more than a century. Croke amassed a fortune in experimental farming at his 6,000-acre spread in Brighton, north of Denver, and in other business ventures, and he built his Capitol Hill mansion in 1891. He had begun his career in the mercantile business, but agriculture had always attracted his interest. He organized the Denver Reservoir and Irrigation Company in conjunction with his farming investment. He was also the head of the Platte Valley Land Company. Croke was elected state senator in 1911. Even during his term, his main political interests involved agriculture and irrigation. Around 1900, the Croke family moved permanently to the Brighton farm, and the mansion was sold to Thomas Patterson, prominent and influential publisher and attorney.

Born in Ireland in 1839, Patterson came to the United States with his parents at a young age. The family lived in New York until moving to Crawfordsville, Indiana, in 1853. Patterson was apprenticed in the newsroom of the *Crawfordsville Review*, then moved on to Indianapolis to continue his career. After serving in the Civil War, he received a law degree from Wabash University and practiced with a partner, J.R. Cowan, until coming west to Colorado in the early 1870s. Once here, he became a partner of Charles Thomas, who had recently set up his law practice in Denver, and for a time specialized in criminal law.

In 1874, Patterson ran for city attorney. He won that election, and, while serving in office, he announced his candidacy for representative to Congress. He won, and it was while he was in Washington that he lobbied for Colorado statehood. In August 1876, Colorado became the thirty-eighth state of the union. Patterson then ran for Colorado's first congressional seat and was sworn into office in 1877. He kept up his partnership with Thomas; the team was well known throughout the state and was immensely successful in resolving mining disputes.

Patterson was a delegate to the National Democratic Conventions of 1876, 1880, 1888, and 1892, and he was a member of the National Democratic Committee from 1874 to 1880. Patterson also continued his practice of criminal law.

He also continued his interest in the newspaper business. He became the owner of the *Denver Times*, and in 1890, he purchased the *Rocky Mountain News*, Denver's popular paper that was founded three decades earlier by William Byers. Patterson became

The Croke/Patterson/Campbell chateau at Eleventh Avenue and Pennsylvania Street.

Author's Collection

a U.S. senator and served from 1901 to 1907. During his term, Patterson became one of the great promoters of the state of Colorado.

At the time Patterson and his family lived in the Eleventh Avenue house, the main floor contained a drawing room, a library, a dining room, and a kitchen, all centered around a large reception hall. Five bedrooms were located on the second floor, with an additional three bedrooms on the third floor, along with a children's playroom. The house was connected to a large stable, which was later used as an automobile garage. The exterior featured an exuberant display of architectural elements, including ornamented parapets and tall towers, a rusticated stone base, and a steep roofline topped with finials and tall chimneys.

The Patterson's only child, a daughter named Margaret, had married Richard C. Campbell. She was a graduate of Bryn Mawr College and was heavily involved in church and social work. The couple remained in the house with her parents.

Senator Patterson died in 1916. The Campbells and their children chose to stay in the house for a number of years before building their own house at the northwest corner of Ninth Avenue and York Street. They lived there until the 1960s, when the residence became offices for the adjacent Botanic Gardens.

In the late 1920s, the Croke/Patterson house was divided into apartments. It was subsequently purchased in the late 1940s by Dr. Arthur Sudan, who had come to Colorado from Chicago and built up a practice in Kremmling. He was the recipient of the American Medical Association "Doctor of the Year" award in 1948.

The house had a number of subsequent owners and has been used as business offices since the early 1970s.

For the past few years, the house has again become a private residence, a turn of events extremely rare in the history of vintage Denver mansions. The new owners have been careful to keep the integrity of

Author's Collection

Detail of the Thomas Patterson house.

the house intact, by working closely with Historic Denver, Inc. and other agencies to ensure the survival of one of a dwindling breed. The house was designated an historic landmark and was placed on the National Register in 1973.

Chapter 37

Owen LeFevre House

1311 York Street

Architects: Kirchner & Kirchner

Built: 1891

Judge Owen LeFevre, judge of the second judiciary district and mayor of Highlands for almost fifty years, was a well known patron of the arts. He bought his massive, 10,000-square-foot house at the northwest corner of Thirteenth Avenue and York Street, in 1896, when the area was considered to be on the edge of town. It was built in 1893 by the firm of Kirchner & Kirchner, for Colonel Charles E. Taylor. The house was constructed of stone and pressed brick and featured a large covered porch surrounding the east and south sides. The reception hall was twelve by eighteen feet and finished in quartered oak. To the left was the drawing room, thirty-two by fifteen feet, also finished in oak. The original dining area was trimmed in poplar. The main floor also contained the library and sitting room. A large stairwell led to the second-floor bedrooms, dressing rooms, and bathrooms, most finished in poplar. The top floor featured a billiards room and storerooms, while the basement contained rooms for laundry and storage, along with a large boiler room.

LeFevre and his wife, Eva French, whom he married in 1871, filled the home with rare and beautiful works of art collected during the family's travels throughout Europe and Asia, where they not only made purchases, but seriously studied the art and cultures of the people of these areas. LeFevre was able to indulge in his artistic interests as a result of great wealth attained through his astute business acumen and naturally shrewd nature.

The Owen LeFevre house has been headquarters for Alcoholics Anonymous for more than fifty years.

Judge LeFevre was born in Ohio in 1848, where he attended grade and preparatory schools. At the age of sixteen, he joined the 154th Regiment of Ohio Volunteers and left the service soon after the war ended. He went back to finish his education at the University of Michigan, where he graduated in 1870. He spent the next two years teaching school and studying law. He completed his law course in 1872 and was admitted to the bar in Ohio shortly afterward. After two years with the firm of McMahon & Houck, he and his wife moved to Denver.

He continued the practice of law and was soon elected mayor of Highlands. He was connected in business matters to many prominent men of the day and was a friend of John Evans, John Evans, Jr., and Harold Kountze. He joined with A.E. Reynolds and Henry Wolcott in the mining business. They had holdings in the Creede area that paid them immense sums through their discovery of silver. They also had other interests in mining and real estate.

LeFevre died in 1921. He was survived by his widow and daughter. Mrs. LeFevre, never one to sit idly by, threw herself headlong into her social and civic work for which she was already well known. She sat on the first board of St. Luke's Hospital and was an active member of the Ladies' Relief Society, an early

Denver charity. She was an original founder of the Charity Organization Society, one of the first charity movements in the country, and was a supporter of Children's Hospital and the Denver Orphan's Home. She held fund-raising events annually for both institutions. She was on the board of directors of the YWCA for many years and was also a member of the Denver Women's Club and the Women's Press Club. Others that benefited from her benevolence were the Florence Crittendon Home for Girls and the Denver Art Museum. When she died at the age of ninety-six in 1948, she was the oldest member of the Community Chest, which later became the United Way.

The house was willed to the Denver District Court. The court, under the direction of Judge Philip Gilliam, sold the mansion to the Denver Chapter of Alcoholics Anonymous for a nominal price. At the closing of the deal, Gilliam wrote a letter to AA officials saying, "I cannot praise Alcoholics Anonymous enough for the wonderful service they have given to the city of Denver, the state and the nation. It would be tragic to have them fail in their endeavor to enlarge their facilities and care for more people who need their help. It is my earnest wish that Alcoholics Anonymous will be able to get the co-operation of the entire city of Denver to expand their operations and carry on their fine work." And so it has been for more than fifty years.

Chapter 38

ISAAC BUSHONG HOUSE

2036 EAST SEVENTEENTH AVENUE

ARCHITECT: GEORGE BETTCHER

BUILT: 1903

The Denver Orphan's Home once had a block all to itself. The home, located at the northeast corner of Sixteenth Avenue and Race Street, was a tall Victorian structure with all the proper elements and fittings, such as shutters, gingerbread trim, bay windows, and a picket fence. Built in 1881, this sturdy brick house was a refuge to the neglected and homeless children of early Denver, and the institution was a pet project of many of Denver's society matrons. The rest of the block was taken up by outdoor play areas, a barn, and other outbuildings. At the turn of the century, the institution moved to new quarters at Colfax and Albion, where it continues today.

The Race Street structure was demolished around 1902 and the block was divided into lots. The first lot to be developed was at the southwest corner of Seventeenth Avenue and Vine Street. Built for Isaac Bushong of gray pressed brick in a modified Romanesque style, with a hipped roof accommodating four dormers and four chimneys, the house was unique in its design and floor plan. The *Denver Times* of May 1903 gave this glowing account: "At the corner of Seventeenth avenue and Vine street is being erected a residence that will be one of the prettiest homes on Capitol Hill. This is the first of the handsome homes to be built on the block formerly used for the Orphan's home, and the thirty lots comprised in the former site of that institution will be built up with residences of like character. While elaborate in conception it is of charming modest beauty so much admired in a home. The deed transferring thirty lots including this site, from Orville L. Dines to I.N. Bushong has been recorded."

The Bushong mansion was built on the site of the former Denver Orphan's Home.

Architect George Bettcher (1862–1952) came to Denver to set up his practice in 1895, and this house was one of his earliest and most ambitious projects in Capitol Hill. He went on to design many other structures, including the Henry Van Schaack residence at 145 Lafayette Street and Stedman School at 2940 Dexter Street.

The exterior of the Bushong house is severe, with only a few arched windows to break the plane. The house was originally constructed with a two-story enclosed porch on the west side and a one-story open porch to the east. Both have been removed. Demolished, also, was a three-car garage on the alley.

The entry door, made of oak, led to a small vestibule with a mosaic marble floor in a Greek key pattern. An inner door, also of oak, led to a central hallway featuring a large brass chandelier that was fitted for both gas and electricity, manufactured at a time when home electricity was still somewhat unreliable. Four cut-glass globes shared the fixture with four gas jets and four electric lights. The staircase to the second floor, lined waist-high with tooled Spanish leather, swept past two large, arched, cut-glass windows on the landing.

The main floor consisted of a large drawing room, a smaller sitting room, a washroom, and a dining room with a combination fireplace and built-in oak cabinetry with glass doors. The drawer pulls of the cabinet were lions' heads of solid brass. A large kitchen was adjacent to the dining room, along with a butler's pantry complete with a long, glass-paneled, floor-to-ceiling china cupboard.

The drawing room featured a columned fireplace of burled maple, and green tiles and a cast-iron hearth. Two cut-glass windows reflected rainbow patterns into the room. The chandelier was brass with five cut-glass globes and a center light. Four bedrooms were located on the second floor, two with fireplaces. One fireplace mantel was made of oak and the other of cherry. The bathroom had a white ceramic floor, a marble sink, and a roomy claw-foot bathtub. The original servants' quarters were located on the third floor, which contained three rooms and a bath, with an attic space above.

The basement contained another bedroom with a fireplace, along with a small bath, a furnace room,

The hallway of the Bushong mansion at the time it was a bed-and-breakfast.

Author's Collection

a laundry, a food pantry, and a coal room. All the doorknobs in the house were of solid brass. The flooring was honey oak throughout.

The house was leased in 1933 by this author's grandparents. They purchased the property in 1936, and it was his childhood home until 1965, when it was sold to an attorney for use as offices. It was sold again in 1994 and enjoyed a short success as a bed-and-breakfast, under the ownership of Dorothy Bowie, at a time when many of the large, older houses in the neighborhood were being converted for the same purpose. Mrs. Bowie recalls: "We began work on the house immediately, as there was a lot to take care of. One of the projects was to expand the first-floor kitchen by knocking out a wall and opening the area to make it more practical. We were careful to try to preserve the integrity of the house, while at the same time making sure it would serve our purpose."

There were a few unexplained events in the house during this period. "A friend who was doing construction work on the terraces directly across Seventeenth came over one day to help us with a project," said Mrs. Bowie. "He and I took the front stairs down to the basement so he could take a look at what I wanted done. I went first, and he followed. Behind us we heard a third set of footsteps, slowly—one after the other. We both turned around to look, and no one was there.

"Another time, my then-husband and I had gone out for the evening. There was no one else staying in the house at the time. When we returned late in the evening, we found the front door ajar, a bottle cap inside the entry, and the alarm system still activated. It had not been set off, and nothing was taken from the house. However, if spirits were indeed roaming around the property, I never once felt scared."

In 1999, the house was sold again, then remodeled and refurbished, and currently it is used for law offices. Over the years, the house has seen duty as a private home, the Mathews School of Music, offices, and apartments. Most of the other houses on the block were built up slowly, between 1905 and 1925. All are part of what is now the Wyman Historic District.

Chapter 39

Raymond House/ Castle Marne

1572 Race Street

Architect: William Lang

Built: 1889

At the corner of Sixteenth Avenue and Race, on Denver's Capitol Hill, a famous old mansion is celebrating its 114th year, having been lovingly restored to its original splendor. The rusticated lava-stone house was built in 1889, amidst the greatest construction boom in Denver's history. The architect was William Lang, the most eclectic architect of the time. Known over the years as the Raymond House and/or The Marne, the house has patiently endured years of treatment "varying from weepy-eyed love to flinty entrepreneurial stewardship" (*Rocky Mountain News*, January 11, 1976).

The Raymond house is one of the most recognized and admired houses in the Wyman Historic District. The house was commissioned by Wilbur S. Raymond at a cost of $40,000 on lots purchased for $15,000, in an age when the average house sold for around $3,500. An article in the *Denver Republican*, dated January 1, 1890, boasted: "The fact that men are able to build and maintain such houses and the further fact that they possess the taste for these elegant domestic surroundings, proves to the world that Denver has reached the social age in which refinement, culture and love of the beautiful stamp the character of the people."

Raymond and his family lived in the house less than a year. He lost the house to creditors in 1891 but continued in the investment business until 1898.

The Wilbur S. Raymond house, now Castle Marne, at the southeast corner of Sixteenth Avenue and Race Street.

The next owner was Colonel James H. Platt. Born of American parents in Canada in 1837, he was educated there and at the University of Vermont. He served in the Civil War and continued in the military after the war's end. From 1870 to 1872, he was secretary of the National Republican Congressional Executive Committee. He was U.S. Representative from Virginia for six terms and served in President Grant's cabinet. He had business interests with John D. Rockefeller, Sr. but sold out in 1885. Platt moved to Denver in 1887 and established the Equitable Accident Insurance Company. He left that business to pursue his interest in the manufacture of paper. In 1890, he began one of the finest paper mills in the world, the Denver Paper Mills Company. When the mill was completed, it was the largest building in Colorado. It was located at West Louisiana Avenue and South Jason Street in an area then known as Manchester.

Detail of one of the fireplaces in the Raymond House/ Castle Marne. This hand-carved dolphin was a symbol of good fortune.

Author's Collection

Platt died under mysterious circumstances while on a family fishing trip near Georgetown in June 1895. He had gone boating by himself and fell into the water and drowned. His widow sold the house the following year. After Platt's death, the mill was sold, and the name was changed to the Rocky Mountain Paper Company. A few other businesses used the building before it was demolished in the 1960s. Its giant smokestack, an area landmark, came down at the same time.

The house next was sold to John T. Mason, who was a founder and first curator of the Denver Museum of Natural History. Mason displayed his world-famous collection of more than 40,000 butterflies and moths in the ballroom on the third floor of the mansion. He donated this collection to the museum in 1918, where it was viewed by thousands over the next few decades. Unfortunately, it is not presently on view. Mason is included among the city's benefactors whose names are permanently recorded in the marble wall of the Greek Amphitheater in Denver's Civic Center Park. His wife, Dora Porter Mason, was the daughter of one of the city's wealthiest and most prominent pioneers, Henry Porter, founder of Porter Hospital.

The house was again sold, this time in 1918 to Mrs. Edwin Van Cise, whose late husband was former head of the Denver Public Utilities Commission. Mrs. Van Cise and her son, Philip, named the mansion "The Marne." It is believed that Philip Van Cise fought in the Battle of the Marne in World War I. He was an attorney for the *Rocky Mountain News* during the famous *Denver Post*/Frederick Bonfils scandal and trial, and as Denver district attorney, he mounted a war against gambling, prostitution, and organized crime. He was also instrumental in the fight against the Ku Klux Klan, which, in the 1920s, had gained a stranglehold on Denver politics, especially within the offices of Mayor Benjamin Stapleton.

Mrs. Van Cise converted the mansion to apartments and lived there until her death in 1937.

Lyle Holland purchased The Marne the following year and lived there for the rest of his life. He was associated with Gus's Bakery and subsequently

Author's Collection

Carved stonework on the exterior of the Raymond House/Castle Marne, the well-known signature of architect William Lang.

conducted his real-estate dealings from the mansion. When he died in 1974, there were many futile attempts made by speculators to develop the property.

The house changed hands again. The new owners, Louise and Richard Dice, attempted to convert the house into three condos, one per floor. From 1979 through 1982, the house served as a processing center for parolees from state penal institutions. The Marne then stood empty and was vandalized until 1988, when the Peiker family purchased the derelict structure. One year later, after an extensive restoration project, the Castle Marne opened as a bed-and-breakfast and fast became one of the most successful of its type in the state.

The Peikers—Jim, Diane, and daughter Melissa Feher-Peiker—are from pioneer Denver families. They support and actively participate in the preservation and restoration of Denver's rich and colorful history. Castle Marne is an official landmark of Denver and is on the National Register of Historic Structures. The Denver Chapter of the American Institute of Architects has noted: "The Castle Marne is truly one of Denver's great architectural legacies."

The house was originally built with two entrances, one facing Race Street and the other facing Sixteenth Avenue. They both led directly to Mr. Raymond's downstairs office, an innovation at the time. The house was one of the first in the neighborhood to have indoor plumbing. The lighting fixtures were both electric and gas, due to the unreliable nature of early electric lighting.

The interior of the house has been remodeled a number of times to accommodate the demands of the different owners. Currently, the main floor consists of the foyer, a formal parlor, a back parlor, a dining room, a kitchen, one bedroom, a two-room suite under construction, and three baths. The second floor has four bedrooms and four baths, and the top floor has four bedrooms, four baths, and a parlor. A gift shop, a business office, a guest office, a game room, and a laundry are located in the lower level.

The interior has been expertly decorated in keeping with the styles of the day, and many fine antiques, some owned by the Peikers for years, grace the rooms. The woodwork throughout the house has been restored, and most of the rooms are finished in tiger-eye oak. Many of the mansion's fireplaces are elaborately carved, with tile surrounds and bevel-glass mirrors. The stairwell landing features a spectacular stained- and cut-glass window in a round peacock pattern. It is the focal point of the entryway. Although most of the original lighting fixtures were removed in the days when the house was used for apartments, the replacement fixtures are sympathetic to the period. A walk through the house gives one the impression of having stepped back in time. The exterior of the house has remained virtually unchanged since it was built, complete with its low stone retaining wall and wrought-iron railing. A large carriage house is located to the east of the mansion.

William Lang, who was responsible for so many distinctive buildings in the Denver area during his career as an architect, left an indelible impression on the city's landscape. Noted mostly for his work in Capitol Hill, he was highly prolific in the late 1880s and early 1890s, and some of his best work survives today. His hallmarks were rusticated stone, sweeping arches, and stonework that was heavily carved. His career suffered greatly after the Panic of 1893, when so many fortunes were lost, and he was left with virtually no clients and no work. He later left the city to live outside of Chicago and fell into a life of alcohol and menial jobs. During a night of binge drinking, he was run down by a train as he was meandering down the tracks—a tragic end to a brilliant career.

In the Castle Marne, you will find the only known sculptured bust of the late architect, masterfully executed in bronze by a former guest.

The Peikers have hosted afternoon teas, intimate wedding receptions, small business meetings, and romantic candlelight dinners. Further information about the mansion can be found on their website: www.castlemarne.com.

Chapter 40

EBEN SMITH HOUSE

1801 YORK STREET

ARCHITECTS: WILLIAM FISHER
& DANIEL HUNTINGTON

BUILT: 1902

T he imposing and, to some, mystifying mansion that stands at the corner of Eighteenth Avenue and York Street has been a local landmark since it was built in 1902. Many of the thousands of commuters who pass by this intersection every day view it with mild curiosity, and the many who have unanswered questions will find some of the answers here.

At the time it was constructed, the house sat at the very edge of the city and had an unobstructed view of City Park. The neighborhood was starting to build up, but it was a slow process, and the owners enjoyed a tranquil atmosphere, almost free of any noise or unexpected intrusion.

The house was built by Eben Smith for his son, Frank Smith. Eben Smith, who was born in Pennsylvania, had gone to California at a young age, lured by the excitement of gold discoveries. After two years of placer mining there, he went to Nevada, and in a few years he owned the largest milling plant in the region. He sold his interests and moved to St. Joseph, Missouri. While there, he met Jerome Chaffee, and the two came to Colorado about 1860. They brought with them the machinery for a stamp mill, which they set up in Lake Gulch in Gilpin County, and there they developed the Bob Tail and Gregory mines. The two were to remain business partners for many years.

The Eben Smith residence, at 1801 York Street.

Eben Smith then developed interests in the Cripple Creek area and was one of the founders, along with David H. Moffat, of the Florence and Cripple Creek Railroad. He also invested in mines in the Leadville area when that industry was booming.

After moving to Denver, he helped found the First National Bank, along with Chaffee, Moffat, and several other businessmen. In 1876, he moved to Boulder. With Chaffee, he developed the famous Caribou Consolidated Mining Company, which became a source of much of his wealth. Smith was head of the company until 1881.

Smith left Boulder and returned to Leadville in 1882, where he managed Moffat's interests on Carbonate Hill. He developed mines there over the next ten years. He also took over the development of other Moffat mines at Creede, Victor, and Summit. He had even more business interests in Oregon, Arizona, and Utah. Through his various enterprises, he became one of the wealthiest men in Colorado.

In 1866, he married Emily Rundel, who later became involved with many charities, including the Denver Orphan's Home, the Old Ladies' Home, and Children's Hospital. The couple had two sons, Lemuel and Frank. The Smiths also had a daughter. Frank Smith was an organizer of the Mine & Smelter Supply Company, which he sold in 1901. He also had investments in mining and real estate.

The edge of City Park was being touted as Denver's answer to Central Park. Many fine homes were being proposed on the west, south, and east sides, and the area boasts many imposing houses to this day, in all styles of architecture. The twenty-room Smith mansion, comprising three stories and a basement, was built of beige brick in what has been described as a French neoclassical style. It also has many Georgian elements.

The entrance opens into a small, curved vestibule that leads to a main hall and a dramatic sweeping staircase. The hall boasts a large brass chandelier that was fitted for both electricity and gas jets. Located on the landing of the staircase are French doors leading to a small outside balcony with wrought-iron railing. The main-floor rooms, spacious and masterfully crafted, are built around the central hall, which is wood paneled about halfway to the ceiling. The upper walls are embellished with heavy plaster ornamentation. The second floor has large bedrooms, many with fireplaces, and a central hall looking down into the open stairwell. The top floor originally contained bedrooms and a huge playroom for the five Smith children. As a whole, the opulent interior shows the finest of craftmanship from the Edwardian era. To the west of the main house is a large, two-story carriage house, first used for horses and buggies and later for automobiles.

Eben Smith left Colorado in the early 1900s to live in California. He made occasional visits to Denver to check on business investments and to visit his daughter, Mrs. Charles Carnahan. It was at her home, at 951 Logan Street, that he died in 1906 at the age of seventy-five.

Frank Smith gave up the house after his divorce from his wife, Josephine, in 1907. The house was next occupied by Genevieve Phipps, estranged wife of millionaire steel man Lawrence Phipps. She later sold the house to Mr. and Mrs. John Anthony Crook. He was president of Denver Steel and Iron Works. Mrs. Crook remodeled the top-floor playroom into one of the grandest ballrooms in the city. It became the scene of some of Denver's most memorable parties. The walls were hand painted with scenes of Europe, and the floor was of solid oak. Seating around the dance floor was upholstered in blue tufted velvet. The ballroom also held a stage at one end to accommodate musicians and for the many theatricals that were held there.

It was also in this house, supposedly, that Miss Anne Evans, daughter of Territorial Governor John Evans, plotted, along with Mrs. Crook, Ida Kruse McFarlane, and other civic-minded matrons, to save the dilapidated Central City Opera House from oblivion. The building, constructed in 1878, had long since seen better days and was being used for storage. The restoration was completed through fund-

raising efforts and some astute business acumen, and the 1932 season opened with a showing of the play *Camille*, starring the famous stage and film actress Lillian Gish. The opera house has remained popular ever since.

After John Crook's death in 1936, his widow occupied the York Street mansion until around 1950, when it was purchased by Laura Mitchell and turned into the Briar Manor boardinghouse. During that period, the mansion was allowed to deteriorate. A leaky roof caused water damage to some walls and to part of the elaborate plasterwork. The interior

Interior of 1801 York Street.
Author's Collection

was remodeled to accommodate paying guests but didn't suffer the severe damage from remodeling experienced by some of the other mansions in Capitol Hill.

In 1971, the Smith house was approved by the Denver Planning Board for designation as a historic landmark by the Denver Landmark Preservation Commission. About that time, the mansion was converted to use for business offices.

By 1985, L. Douglas Hoyt, real-estate man and attorney, had bought the house and given it a million-dollar restoration job. Oak paneling that had been painted over was stripped to its original surface; repairs were made to the ornamental plasterwork throughout the house; many of the brass and copper lighting fixtures were refitted; and damage to the roof and exterior facing was repaired. The one concession to modern times was the installation of an elevator.

In 1990, the 10,000-square-foot mansion was placed on the market and is now occupied by the law offices of Silver & DeBoskey.

Ralph Voorhees House

Looming large above the shops, strip malls, and fast-food restaurants of West Colfax is the castlelike roofline of one of Denver's monuments to the Gilded Age. It is also one of architect William Lang's best surviving examples. It has a long and varied history. Its builder, Ralph Voorhees, real-estate investor and promoter, was born in New York in 1855. With only a grammar-school education, he found work in a wholesale grocery. He arrived in Denver in 1880 with little money and big ideas. He found work as a ticket agent for the Denver & Rio Grande Western Railroad, and in the mid-1880s he established his own real-estate office. Eventually, he gained extensive land holdings throughout Colorado, particularly in west Denver.

Voorhees was a member of the Colorado legislature and was also a founder of Colorado Women's College in east Denver. As regional head of the Sons of the Revolution, Voorhees was one of the originators of Flag Day. It was started in Denver and eventually became a national holiday. He was elected representative of Arapahoe County in the Eighth General Assembly in 1890, about the same time he built his elaborate mansion on Stuart Street. He was also responsible for the construction of four other large houses on Stuart Street, between Colfax and West Fourteenth Avenue, and two on Raleigh Street, one block east. All but one of these houses are still in existence and have been well maintained.

The Ralph Voorhees residence, one of many designed by Denver architect William Lang in the 1400 block of Stuart Street.

To promote this neighborhood, Voorhees was instrumental in the building of a viaduct from Larimer Street to Federal Boulevard, across the railroad tracks—a path that was previously traveled with some difficulty.

Voorhees lived at 1471 Stuart Street, the largest and most opulent of the group. The *Western Architect and Building News* described the house, built on five lots, as being "constructed of rusticated white lava stone, with a main hall of quarter sawed golden oak, with highly carved paneling." The gardens to the south were adjacent to a detached three-car garage.

A drive and portico were located on the north side. The parlor and library were finished in cherry wood, and the dining room was of Georgia curled maple. The second floor and attic were done in black ash and Georgia curled maple. Plate-glass, bevel-plate, and cut-jewel windows were custom-made in Chicago.

The eighteen-room, three-story house was originally lighted by kerosene and was wired for electricity around the turn of the century. The main-floor rooms are accessed from a central hall, with its large, open stairwell, heavy wood paneling, hall seating, and two small, arched, stained-glass

Stairwell of the Ralph Voorhees mansion.

Double windows by the entrance to the Voorhees residence.

windows. All the large doorways opening from the hallway have pocket doors that slide on casters. On the stairwell landing is a huge, arched, beveled, stained-glass window. Also on the landing is a red velvet window seat.

The drawing room boasts a carved wood mantel, with a fireplace surround of Colorado white marble. This room also features two large windows, the upper portions done in stained glass in typical elaborate Victorian design. An adjacent library measures a generous fifteen by sixteen feet, and the adjoining parlor has a hand-carved wood fireplace mantel. Both are lighted with large brass chandeliers.

The dining room is paneled waist-high with Georgia curly pine and features a beveled- and stained-glass window. This room also has a hand-carved wood fireplace, along with exotic Oriental wallpaper that may be original to the house. The

east wall has built-in storage drawers. The adjacent kitchen is generously proportioned and was originally paneled with Texas pine. A butler's pantry, off the kitchen, is five by fifteen feet and has a long, floor-to-ceiling china cupboard and built-in drawers.

One of the most remarkable features of the house is the solarium, which was added to the house around the turn of the century. Large, comfortable, and bright, it also has a large stained-glass window above the French doors that connect this room with the library. Another door opens to the south gardens.

The second floor contains a fifteen-by-nineteen-foot master bedroom, with a carved fireplace in one corner of the room. A guest bedroom has two large windows topped with beveled and stained glass. A south bedroom has a view of the gardens and the solarium. Adjacent is what was originally a sewing room. The front bedroom is octagonal and measures about thirteen by fifteen feet. The north bedroom measures fourteen by seventeen feet.

The second-floor bathroom contains a bathtub that measures almost six feet and a marble-top sink. This room also has a porcelain footbath and a pull-chain toilet.

Located in the basement is a laundry, a pantry with shelving, and a "throne" toilet, which is no longer in operation. The present furnace room was updated a few years ago and contains twin forced-air furnaces. The original furnace room measured ten by twenty feet, and had an adjoining coal and wood room. The floors throughout the entire house are of maple.

Voorhees, his wife Fannie, and their children moved from the house in 1907. Voorhees was living at 1543 Washington Street when he died in 1936.

The Stuart Street house changed hands a number of times. It was purchased two years ago by Wade Eldridge, attorney and avid motorcyclist, who works out of his offices in the house. "I was looking around Capitol Hill for a suitable house and bought the Voorhees property when it came on the market," he explained. "We are currently working on more improvements, including remodeling of the main-floor kitchen."

The house has been adequately maintained over the years, compared to many others of the same era that suffered abuse, neglect, and division into apartments and business offices. The integrity of the house remains intact, and it is listed in the National Register of Historic Places of the U.S. Department of the Interior, as was recommended by the Colorado Historical Society.

Another William Lang–designed house in the 1400 block of Stuart Street.

Author's Collection

John Mouat House / Lumber Baron Inn

2555 West Thirty-Seventh Avenue

Architect: Unknown

Built: 1890

M any people happen upon one of northeast Denver's finest Victorian homes quite by accident. Standing like a citadel for well over a century a block south of Thirty-Eighth Avenue at the northeast corner of Bryant Street in the Highlands District is the former residence of lumber-mill owner John Mouat (pronounced Mow-it). He supplied lumber for many of the city's early houses and commercial buildings and was a vice-president of the North Side Building and Loan Company. His lumber company flourished, and he was eventually bought out by the Hallack-Howard Lumber Company.

He built this Queen Anne–style, 10,000-square-foot mansion, boasting elaborate woodwork in cherry, sycamore, oak, and walnut supplied by his company, and used it as a means to promote his business to his many guests. A carved stone inset on the west side of the house features thistle and woodworking tools, noting the owner's profession and Scottish heritage.

Mouat lived in this house until around 1902, when he moved to Fifth Avenue and Pearl Street in central Denver. He soon retired from business and moved to southern California. The house on West Thirty-Seventh Avenue next became the Denver Business University, from 1904 to 1909.

By the 1920s, it had become a multiunit residence, and home to the Hiram Fowler family. Over the years, it was divided into

The John Mouat residence in Highlands, now the Lumber Baron Inn.

twenty-three separate apartments. The Fowlers and their son, James, had ties to the house for the next sixty years. James Fowler was a well-known Denver Socialist and founder of the Denver Urban Garden movement. He eventually became full owner of the mansion.

The house has a wood-paneled vestibule that leads into a roomy entry hall with a finely carved oak staircase, open at the second level. The main floor consists of a parlor, a library, a dining room, a kitchen, and a pantry. The second floor has five guest bedrooms. The house is topped with what was once the city's largest private ballroom.

Over the many decades of its use as apartments, the house suffered a great deal of abuse. Much of the interior was damaged due to reckless remodeling, and eight of the hand-carved fireplace mantels were

stolen, along with many of the original stained-glass windows. The house was also allowed to deteriorate structurally, and the yard was virtually ignored. The mansion sat for years with cracked windows, sagging steps, and peeling paint. Tenants destroyed or defaced much of the interior of the house over a period of years.

It also carries tragic tales, among them a double homicide. In October 1970, at the height of the hippie era, two teenage girls were murdered in the house. They were found by a friend, and speculation was that they were killed by someone they knew. Although the case is revived from time to time, it remains unsolved to this day. As a result, rumors have circulated over the years that the house is haunted.

By 1991, the house was in terrible shape and had been condemned by the city when an enterprising young man named Walt Keller stepped in. He purchased the mansion on April Fool's Day of that year for the nominal price of $80,000, with the intent of cleaning it up and restoring it to its original splendor. Keller has a long history in the area. Born in St. Paul, Minnesota, he moved with his family to Denver when he was six months old. He has lived in the Highlands neighborhood ever since, attending North High School and teaching there for three years before taking on the inn.

The house features beautifully carved woodwork, bevel-glass windows, large-pocket doors, and high ceilings. Most of these ceilings and many walls were specially decorated by the wallpaper firm of Bradbury & Bradbury of California. The wallpaper treatments are not only excellent examples of the wallpapering art but are authentic to the era. Two of the light fixtures are from the Tabor Opera House in Leadville, Colorado.

The top-floor ballroom has a fireplace reputedly from the old David Moffat mansion, which was at one time located on Eighth Avenue and Grant Street in Capitol Hill. The entire floor of this room was salvaged from the high school gym in Chappell,

Detail of the Lumber Baron Inn.
Author's Collection

Interior of the Lumber Baron Inn.

Nebraska. The floor, made of first-grade maple, once hosted the Nebraska state basketball champions during its previous life.

The exterior of the mansion was in bad shape when Keller took over, and much restoration work had to be done, including the complete replacement of the wraparound porch, which was missing by the mid-1940s. The new porch is very close to what would have been in place originally.

The house has won awards due to the enormous cost and exacting nature of the restoration work. It placed second nationally by the National Trust for Historic Preservation, garnering the Great American Home Award. More than $1 million has been spent to bring the mansion up to its current standard.

The mansion is available for overnight or long-term guests, for weddings, for murder mysteries, and for business meetings.

Chapter 43

MARCUS POMEROY HOUSE

2949 WEST THIRTY-SEVENTH AVENUE

ARCHITECT: J.C. CASPER

BUILT: CIRCA 1882

One of the most unlikely mansion builders in the city, specifically in the Highlands area, was Marcus M. "Brick" Pomeroy, a writer, lecturer, editor, spiritualist, and entrepreneur whose plan to build a railroad tunnel underneath the Continental Divide foreshadowed David H. Moffat's plan for a transcontinental railroad route by years.

Pomeroy was born in Elmira, New York, in 1833, the son of a watchmaker. He left home at the age of seventeen and traveled to Corning, where he joined the staff of the *Journal*. A few years later, he started his own newspaper, the *Sun*. He moved to Wisconsin in 1857 and established the *La Crosse Democrat*, which eventually reached a circulation of 100,000. That same year, he started the *New York Democrat* and *Pomeroy's Democrat*, which he continued in Chicago five years later. After a few reverses in his career, he left for Colorado, where he used his promotional skills to the fullest.

Early on, Pomeroy was a mover and shaker in the promotion of a young Denver. He was a businessman who felt deeply that the city was waylaid without a direct railroad route to the west. In 1884, he started the Atlantic-Pacific Railway Tunnel Company to bore a tunnel for commercial and transportation purposes through the Continental Divide. At that time, railroad lines either went north through Wyoming or south along the Rio Grande tracks. Pomeroy garnered enough interest in the project from a number of big-league financial backers, mainly through his theory that while boring through

The Marcus Pomeroy mansion was one of north Denver's most spectacular sights.

the mountain, enough silver and gold ore deposits would be discovered to make the venture not only solid but more than worthwhile. The company secured a bond of $2 million by deeding the company to a trustee. The dangerous, tedious work was soon begun. The proposed tunnel was to be 25,000 feet long, running underneath Gray's Peak and Torrey's Peak, near Loveland Pass. By 1892, the drillers had only bored through from the east a distance of al-most 4,000 feet and almost 1,500 feet from the west. The work was to carry on, day and night, until it came to a screeching halt during the Silver Panic of 1893, a panic that was to bring thousands of investors, speculators, and businessmen to their financial knees. The drilled-out caverns lay hollow and the machinery sat silent. The mountain seemed to resist the attempts to violate its core. Through the years, many meager plans have been made to complete this

tunnel, all to naught, and it sits to this day, openings overgrown with weeds and brush, a symbol of lofty ideals and hard realities.

Pomeroy gave up. He returned to Elmira to publish a political journal. Some of his more significant writings were a collection of his newspaper articles, among which were "Sense," 1868; "Nonsense," 1868; "Gold-Dust," 1871; and "Home Harmonies," 1876. He enjoyed a wide reputation as a journalist until his death in 1896.

Pomeroy built this rather incredible house at West Thirty-Seventh Avenue at Federal Boulevard in the early 1880s, when Federal was no more than a lonely country road. The house was described in the local newspapers as a French villa, constructed of silver-bearing rock and pressed brick, and it featured every modern convenience of the day. The barn, which was more luxurious than most homes in the city, was used to house his $3,000 team and six fine carriages. He was also a poultry farmer and built an elaborate henhouse on the property that cost more than $3,000. Each hen was provided with its own private "sitting" room. The house featured many spacious rooms, with wide halls extending the length of the first and second stories and floors of patterned tiles. It boasted its own theater in the attic, which was fitted with a stage, dressing rooms, and a drop curtain. This room also was used as an art gallery and for dancing. Pomeroy used this theater as a backdrop for his lectures on politics and spiritualism. Next to the house was another structure, built in the style of a Swiss chalet, with a conservatory fronting it.

Pomeroy owned this house until the mid-1890s. Around the turn of the century, it became the Anna Belle Lenox Home and Nursery for Orphaned Children. It continued at that location for the next three decades.

In 1935, Pomeroy's daughter from one of his three marriages had occasion to be in Denver from Ithaca, New York. Her name was Mrs. Douglas Card, and she had been born shortly after the death of her father. She took a tour through the old mansion where she had spent her very earliest childhood. As she strolled through the house with a friend, she inspected the

old woodwork and outdated fixtures. That same year, this house that had attracted so much attention, first as a showplace and later as a hulking relic of bygone times, was wrecked along with the henhouse, the barn, and other outbuildings, to make way for a filling station. The property is used in that capacity today. For the thousands of people who drive by this intersection every day, there is nothing left to indicate the existence of this vanished symbol of Denver's colorful past.

Chapter 44

JOHN HINDRY HOUSE

5500 WASHINGTON STREET

ARCHITECT: UNKNOWN

BUILT: 1873

E very city boasts of a haunted house, and Denver is no exception. Rumors have floated around for years about strange doings in and around some of the more well-known houses, such as the Croke-Patterson castle at Eleventh Avenue and Pennsylvania Street, or the old Bombay Club, at 1128 Grant Street, former home of Governor James Peabody. But no house in Denver was more suited to the task than that of John Hindry, early lumber baron, sewer contractor, and eccentric, who built his fifteen-room Victorian pile high on a hill in north Denver, overlooking the city. The house, built in 1873 in the Italianate style, was located then at Watervliet Avenue, between Cliffors and Mustaine streets. The address was later renamed 5500 North Washington Street. It was located in the center of Globeville, so-named for the Globe Smelter that was built close by a few years later. Trouble was brewing by 1897 when Hindry filed suit against the smelter for ruining his house and property with heavy fumes from its smokestacks. He declared that his land was worth $50,000, with improvements of $100,000, and that it was subsequently worth only $50,000 because of the damage from the smoke and fumes. He charged that the fumes killed his grass, bushes, and trees, as well as his horses, as they grazed on the tainted property. Similar charges included that the house itself was uninhabitable and that even the carpets and lace curtains were being eaten away by the noxious fumes. Hindry ultimately lost his case, but trouble was still brewing behind his closed doors.

Hindry's wife died, leaving him alone on the property, far from the center of town and isolated from his neighbors. Three times he was robbed, and the police advised him that since he lived in such a lonely spot, it would be safer to move closer to town. He resisted. He noticed that every time a thief entered the residence, it was through one certain window on the front porch. He decided to spring a trap and purchased a shotgun. He loaded it with buckshot, then affixed the gun to a table, pointing toward the window. To this he tied a cord to the trigger, then he ran the cord to the floor and across the room to the windowsill. When the window was opened, the cord would pull the trigger.

It wasn't long before he returned home after an overnight trip into town to find his first victim. When police arrived, he told them that he was afraid of remaining in the house the previous night, as he was hard of hearing and thought someone might enter the house and kill him. He had gone to the Windsor Hotel, where he spent the night. This was the first of three victims of his rigged rifle. Two others followed in short order before word got out to the general public, and any efforts to rob him suddenly stopped. But it wasn't long before Hindry was a victim of his own paranoia. One night, after coming back in from checking for prowlers, he accidentally tripped the cord and was shot with his own gun. He survived and moved to California, where he died of old age in 1906.

The mansion, by now run down and surrounded by barren grounds, sat boarded up for more than a decade before the Bomareto family purchased it in 1921. The tower had been removed and the porches sagged. Neighbors and passersby reported strange doings on the isolated property, although police checking on these reports rarely found anything out of the ordinary. Local children told each other tales of strange sightings and unearthly noises coming from the place. Police, however, did find trouble in 1961 when they raided the house on a Sunday night and found an illegal "bottle club" being run by one of the occupants, Frank Bomareto. Fourteen men and one woman were charged with the illegal sale of liquor and of operating a gambling house. Customers from as far away as Aurora traveled to the house to get drinks at a cheap price and to try their luck at the tables. The operation was quickly shut down and all were charged.

That was far from the end of the misery that seemed to envelope the old house like a shroud. The following year, the mansion was gutted by a devastating fire, and Frank Bomareto barely escaped with his life. When the four fire trucks arrived on the property, the house was already a blazing inferno. Bomareto, who was alone in the house at the time, told the fire inspectors that he was "blown out of bed" and found the house fully engulfed. He jumped through a window from the second floor and landed on a ledge before calling for help. His brother, who lived in a house nearby, heard his screams and came to help.

By daybreak, the mansion was almost completely burned, with only a few smoldering walls left standing. The cause of the fire was never fully explained, although faulty electrical wiring was not ruled out. The surviving walls eventually collapsed, and today there is no trace of what was once one of north Denver's finest Victorian residences.

Denver Public Library Western History Collection

Exterior of the John Hindry residence.

Chapter 45

SHANGRI-LA

150 SOUTH BELLAIRE STREET

ARCHITECT: RAYMOND HARRY ERVIN

BUILT: 1938

Over the past six decades, tourists and locals alike have expressed curiosity about the imposing white house high on a hill above busy Colorado Boulevard, at the juncture of Leetsdale Drive and Alameda Avenue. Some view it with a faint familiarity, while others are struck with its stark design—something very reminiscent of the movies of the 1930s. This art-deco masterpiece with streamline detailing was indeed built during that period, and those who saw the 1937 film *Lost Horizon* will remember the monastery of the High Lama, designed for the film by Stephen Gooson. This same style was used heavily in other films of the period and was extremely popular in everything from architecture to furniture to household appliances. Variations of the style flourished through the 1940s and into the 1950s.

This house was built in 1938 in an area of Hilltop now known as Shangri-La Heights. Harry Huffman, Denver theater owner and film promoter, liked the area and the view from the hill and decided to build there. Huffman began his long career as a registered pharmacist and opened his own pharmacy at West Colfax and Lipan in the early 1900s. He became intrigued with the new "moving pictures" that were rapidly gaining in popularity, and in 1909 he opened a nickelodeon, the Bide-A-Wee, next door to his pharmacy. His drugstore clerks did double duty as singers in his new theater.

His venture was successful, and in 1912, he purchased the Bluebird Theater, at 3317 East Colfax. In 1926, he built the Aladdin Theater

The sleek lines of Shangri-La make it one of the best examples of its style in the region.

at 2000 East Colfax, which was one of Denver's premiere first-run theaters. It was here, in 1927, that the city experienced its first taste of the "talkies" with the showing of Al Jolson's *The Jazz Singer*. The Aladdin was widely known for its sumptuous fittings and elaborate decorations, including jade-green plush carpeting, a bubbling fountain, Oriental murals, and twinkling lights that imitated stars across the broad expanse of the theater ceiling.

Huffman eventually acquired more theaters, including the American, the Rialto, the Tabor, and the Broadway, all located downtown. He also bought an interest in the lucrative RKO-Orpheum circuit. He operated all of these theaters until 1937, when the Fox-Intermountain Theater Corporation acquired the contracts, keeping Huffman on as general manager. At one time, Huffman was also manager of the Paramount and Denver theaters.

In 1950, he bought the KLZ radio station and later applied for a license to start a television station, which became KLZ-TV. It debuted in 1953 and was later sold to Time-Life, Inc. Huffman was a director of the American National Bank and was also a founder of the Denver Convention and Visitors Bureau.

Huffman purchased this site in the mid-1930s. The property itself was once part of a large tract of land owned by John Leet, who started the subdivision then known as Leetsdale Farms. At the time of Huffman's purchase, the site was in the country.

Lost Horizon was shown at Huffman's theaters, and his wife, Christine, was enamored with what she saw. When Mr. Huffman decided to build his house, he commissioned architect Raymond Harry Ervin to draw up the plans. Ervin worked with a model of the movie's version to get the proper feel for layout and dimensions. Huffman and his wife wanted a place to not only relax and spend quiet evenings together, but to be able to entertain on a grand scale if they wanted. The house became one of the city's social centers, and Mrs. Huffman was a renowned hostess. She decorated the house elaborately for holidays and special occasions, and many important figures of the entertainment and business worlds were guests of the couple.

The 8,000-square-foot home offered an unparalleled view of the Front Range when it was first built. The property originally sat on five acres, with the front lawn sloping gently westward toward Leetsdale Drive. The house, white with gleaming silver

trim and accents, has thirteen rooms, with a two-story art-deco entryway. The original address to the house was numbered 13 Leetsdale Drive. Thirteen happened to be considered a lucky number by Mr. Huffman.

What was once the home's sloping west lawn was subdivided by developer John Chapin, beginning in 1962. The drive is now lined with upscale homes, including Cableland, built by Bill Daniels, the "Father of Cable TV." It was built to host his many clients and quickly became a center of activity. The house was filled with the latest technological advancements related to television and communications. He had a suite of rooms upstairs at his disposal. After Daniels's death, Cableland was given to the city of Denver as the official mayor's residence.

The rest of the neighborhood has changed drastically since Shangri-La was built. Colorado Boulevard, once a relatively quiet street, is now a major thoroughfare and important commercial street. Adjacent from Shangri-La is the Glendale shopping district. All of Hilltop, to the east, has been built up with residences.

The circular drive to the mansion is now known as Shangri-La Drive. The entrance to Shangri-La fronts Bellaire Street. The house offers a view of Burns Park and its sculpture garden, with the Front Range as its backdrop. The park was donated to the city by real-estate agent Franklin Burns when Huffman bought the property to build Shangri-La.

After Huffman's death in 1969, the house went to his relatives, who, in turn, sold it to twenty-one-year old bachelor David Rumbough, son of actress Dina Merrill and stepson of actor Cliff Robertson. He was also the grandson of Marjorie Meriweather Post, Washington and Palm Beach socialite and heiress to the Post cereal fortune. Rumbough had been attending the University of Denver and had taken a tour through the house when it was featured among the Designer's Showhouses, a benefit for the Children's Hospital Fund. Nearly 10,000 people had toured the house in a one-month period. He liked what he saw and purchased the house from Huffman's nieces. During his pre-sale inspections,

he created a stir for members of the Children's Hospital Auxiliary who were staffing the tour. He arrived once by motorcycle, once on a bicycle, and another time in a bright red Ferrari.

After only four years, the young Rumbough decided to put the house up for sale and move south to Castle Rock. While the house was on the market, Rumbough was killed in a boating accident off the shore of East Hampton, New York.

The house was then purchased by Barry and Arlene Hirschfeld. Hirschfeld is the owner of A.B. Hirschfeld Press, founded by his grandfather in 1907. He has long been involved in the printing business. He also has interests in real estate, especially in the Cherry Creek and central Denver areas. A.B. Hirschfeld served fourteen years in the state legislature, followed by six years in the Colorado Senate. He was also co-owner of the Denver Bears baseball team and the Denver Broncos. Barry and his father Edward are inductees into the Colorado Tourism Hall of Fame. All three were inducted into the Colorado Business Hall of Fame in February 2004. Barry is a member of several boards, and the Hirschfelds, both native Denverites, are prominent in civic affairs. Arlene has been an active volunteer throughout most of her adult life. The Hirschfelds' community involvement is well known.

The Hirschfelds had been living in the Cherry Creek area, and both had known Shangri-La as children. "I used to trick-or-treat here, and I remember the butler coming to the door to hand out Halloween candy," said Mrs. Hirschfeld. "I'd peek into the house to catch a glimpse of Mr. and Mrs. Huffman playing cards. We decided to buy the house because we both were familiar with it, liked it, and also liked the neighborhood."

Very few changes have been made to the house over the last three decades, and the integrity of its architecture remains intact. It is one of the best examples of its architectural style in the region.

Chapter
46

NOTABLE SURVIVORS

WILLIAM BYERS/WILLIAM EVANS HOUSE

Author's Collection

The William Byers/William Evans house, with the Denver Art Museum in the background.

The dark-red, Italian-style mansion that sits at West Thirteenth Avenue and Bannock Street, nestled next to the imposing Denver Art Museum, has been a landmark for well over a century. Built originally for William Byers (1831–

1903), owner and editor of the *Rocky Mountain News*, it was later remodeled and expanded by its subsequent owner, William Gray Evans, son of Colorado Governor John Evans and a major investor in the Denver Tramway Company.

Byers had helped develop Denver in its formative years by bringing in mail delivery and telegraph lines and helping to write the state's constitution. He was also a founder of the University of Denver.

He moved to this location with his wife Elizabeth from his home at the northeast corner of Colfax Avenue and Sherman Street in the early 1880s. He later moved from the Bannock Street address to a new stone mansion on grounds that took up the entire block at South Pearl Street and Bayaud Avenue.

There, Byers and his wife entertained quietly in an almost pastoral setting. After the Byers' deaths, the house was torn down to make way for Byers Junior High School.

The Evans family was one of the state's most prominent, giving their time and money to many worthy causes, including the University of Denver and the Central City Opera House. The house is open to the public.

PETER McCOURT HOUSE

Author's Collection

Peter McCourt, prominent theater manager and brother of Baby Doe Tabor, lived in this house on East Eighth Avenue, one of many in the area he called home in the early 1900s.

Denver to this day has some examples of early architecture on a grand scale. Among the most prominent is the former Peter McCourt residence, at 555 East Eighth Avenue, one of a number of houses he either owned or rented in Denver. McCourt was the brother of Elizabeth "Baby Doe" McCourt Tabor. This is purportedly the only house still in existence in Denver where the Tabors actually lived, though for a very short while.

Peter McCourt became interested in Colorado's mining boom and settled in Leadville in the 1870s.

There he met Horace Tabor, and McCourt was soon made manager of Tabor's new opera house, located in downtown at the southwest corner of Sixteenth Street and Curtis. Until he died in 1929, McCourt was involved in all aspects of Denver's entertainment business, managing not only the Tabor Grand Opera House, but the popular Broadway Theater at 1756 Broadway as well. McCourt later purchased the Tabor Grand and saw it through some of its finest days. He also booked some of the more famous names in stage and film, bringing them to a celebrity-starved city. He later took up residence in the former home of Katherine O'Connor, daughter of J.K. Mullen, at 860 Pennsylvania Street, now demolished.

John Brisben Walker House

Author's Collection

The John Brisben Walker residence in northwest Denver remains much as it was when it was originally built.

The home of John Brisben Walker is located at 3520 Newton Street. Walker made his first fortune by buying the struggling *Cosmopolitan Magazine* and selling it later to William Randolph Hearst at a staggering profit. Brisben made a second fortune in real estate, was a promoter of Red Rocks Park, and a developer of the town of Morrison, Colorado.

Walker envisioned a summer White House in the hills above Denver, and in 1911, he hired Jacques Benedict to design a twenty-two-room stone castle to be built on a cliff high above Bear Creek Canyon. Walker had solicited donations from the public for the project, but funds were slow to come in. He decided to build the foundation with his own money and was unsuccessful in raising more than a little of the additional funding; it therefore sat untended for many years. In 1927, a violent storm hit the area, and Walker's house was destroyed by lightning. The foundation for the summer White House was also destroyed.

In the 1880s, Walker built the so-called Castle of Commerce at Riverfront Park near the Sixteenth Street viaduct in the Platte Valley, and he oversaw the erection of a grandstand and a large racetrack nearby. Riverfront Park was one of the city's first amusement parks, which Walker owned.

The Newton Street house, built in 1885, was rarely used by Walker, who spent a great deal of time traveling, especially to New York. The house occupied an area known as Berkeley Farm, a tract of more than 1,000 acres that Walker owned and operated as a working farm and dairy. The area was built up slowly with residences. The entrance to Walker's house, which faces west, originally faced opposite to Meade Street. Newton was not a through street from Thirty-Fifth Avenue to Thirty-Sixth Avenue as late as 1905.

Walker sold the Newton Street house around the turn of the century. It has been occupied by a number of families and has been designated a Denver Landmark.

John Brisben Walker died in 1935.

WILLIAM WHITEHEAD HOUSE

Author's Collection

Exterior of the William Whitehead Mansion.

The Queen Anne–style residence of William Whitehead, at 1128 Grant Street, was designed by Frank Edbrooke around 1890. Whitehead was a prominent physician and one-time head of the Colorado Medical Society. In 1903, the mansion became the home of Governor James Peabody, who used it as the official governor's mansion throughout his term. The house subsequently became apartments, and a number of restaurants came and went over the years, including the Carriage Inn and the Bombay Club. It now houses offices.

DENNIS SHEEDY HOUSE

Author's Collection

Dennis Sheedy's mansion at Eleventh Avenue and Grant, later the Fine Arts Building.

Dennis Sheedy lived at 1115 Grant Street when that avenue was a grand boulevard. Sheedy was an organizer of the Colorado National Bank and a builder of the Holden and Globe smelters. He also invested in railroads and cattle ranching and had many real-estate dealings. He was a founder of the Denver Dry Goods Company. This house, designed by E.T. Carr in 1892, reflected his taste and the taste of the times in general, with big rooms, expensive woodwork throughout, and a large lot to denote the importance of the owner who dwelt within.

The main floor contained a drawing room, a reception room, and dining and smoking rooms. The main hall was entered through a set of double doors, the outer doors being set with beveled plate glass. The doors were originally protected by an electrified iron grill. The main hall was twenty-six by sixteen feet, and finished in quartered oak. The ceilings on all floors were heavily paneled.

The drawing room was originally decorated in the Louis XIV style. The walls were covered in panels of blue silk in a flower pattern. The ceiling was painted in sky blue, with cupids and garlands of flowers. The reception room was finished in bird's-eye maple, with walls covered in silk. The dining room had wainscoting and walls covered in silk, with scenes of fish and game. The ceiling was paneled in red quarter oak.

Upstairs were seven bedrooms. Queen Anne was an extremely popular style of the 1890s, and this was reflected in many of the houses built in Denver during that time. Various examples still exist in older sections of the city.

After Sheedy's death in the 1920s, the house became a conservatory of fine arts, later sponsored by Helen Bonfils, with studios for voice training, piano, violin, and cello, and space set aside for painting, sculpting, and other plastic arts. It now houses private offices.

WALTER DUNNING HOUSE

Author's Collection

The Walter Dunning residence, at 1200 Pennsylvania Street.

The Walter Dunning residence, built at 1200 Pennsylvania Street of gray lava stone in 1889–1890, featured leaded and stained-glass windows, heavy woodwork throughout, large rooms on the main floor, and a third-floor ballroom. The house, designed by architect William Lang, was sold to James Benedict, a local attorney. Walter S. Cheesman, Denver railroad man, real-estate tycoon, financier, major owner of the monopolistic Denver Union Water Company, and namesake of Cheesman Park, lived here for a short period before dying in the house in 1907. The house changed hands a number of times, and by the 1930s, it was being used as a boardinghouse, called The Graystone. It was remodeled for apartments by the early 1950s. Lee Rudofsky, a Denver realtor, bought the property in 1964 and converted the house for office use. It has been an historic landmark since 1975 and is used for offices to this day.

WILLIAM FRIEDMAN HOUSE

Author's Collection

Castle-like exterior of 733 East Eighth Avenue.

This Flemish-style castle, of dark red brick and high, stepped gables, was built around 1900 at 733 East Eighth Avenue and has had a long connection to the church. Its earliest history is sketchy, but in the 1930s, it was the home of Rabbi William Friedman, leader of Denver's Temple Emanuel and a co-founder of National Jewish Hospital for Consumptives. The hospital treated, for free, many sufferers of tuberculosis and other lung ailments and has garnered a countrywide reputation for excellence in its treatment of its patients. Friedman, born in Chicago in 1868, came to Denver in 1889 to head the newly established temple.

Young, charismatic, and enthusiastic, Friedman quickly gained a large following and was instrumental in establishing charity organizations across the city. He was also active in interdenominational work. He served as chairman, and later as president, of National Jewish Hospital. Friedman died in 1944. The house changed hands a few times, and in the 1970s, it became the home of Carl Frey, Eighth Bishop of the Episcopal Diocese. Television actress Ann B. Davis, best known for her role as Alice on "The Brady Bunch," lived here for a few years as a ministry member. By the 1980s, the house had multiple tenants, and in the last decade it has been used for business offices.

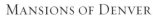

OSCAR MALO HOUSE

Author's Collection

Exterior of the Oscar Malo residence at Eighth Avenue and Pennsylvania Street, adjacent to the Governor's Mansion.

The 15,000-square-foot Malo house, long a neighbor of the Grant/Humphreys and Boettcher mansions, was built in 1921 by Oscar Malo, Denver banker and husband of Edith Mullen, daughter of J.K. Mullen of the Colorado Milling and Elevator Company, for whom Malo worked. The twenty-three-room landmark mansion, designed by architect Harry Manning in the Spanish Colonial Revival style, features spacious main-floor rooms, including a heavily paneled library. The house, at 500 East Eighth Avenue, was deeded to the Denver Archdiocese of the Catholic Church by Malo before he died in 1965, in keeping with the Mullen family's devotion to the Catholic Church over the years. The church, however, never found a use for the mansion, and the house changed hands a number of times. It was used in the 1980s by Swanee Hunt, daughter of oil billionaire H.L. Hunt, who operated her charitable organizations out of the house.

MOSES HALLETT HOUSE

Author's Collection

The Moses Hallett house, at Ninth Avenue and Logan Street, has been a private residence, a rooming house, apartments, and offices.

This imposing landmark mansion at 900 Logan Street was built in the 1890s for Judge Moses Hallett, who moved to Colorado from the Midwest as a man in his thirties in 1860 to form a law practice. Hallett was appointed Chief Justice of the Territory of Colorado in 1866 by then-President Andrew Johnson. He continued to practice in the legal field well after Colorado joined the Union in 1876. The following year, President Grant appointed Judge Hallett to the U.S. District Court for Colorado, and he remained in that position until his retirement in 1906. Hallett became particularly adept at solving complex legal problems pertaining to the mining industry at a time when Colorado

mines were producing at a peak rate. He frequently traveled to the camps of Leadville, Cripple Creek, and Creede to oversee disputes between management and labor that naturally arose in the state's fledgling industry.

In 1892, he became professor of American Constitution Law at the University of Colorado at Boulder. He was also sought after as an expert in the field of water law.

The sprawling thirty-room Hallett mansion, constructed of dark red brick, featured spacious rooms built around a large central hall. Hand-carved

woodwork appeared throughout the house, and custom-made lighting fixtures were fitted for both gas jets and electric wiring. A large drawing room, a dining room, and a library were found on the main floor, while the upstairs contained eight bedrooms and three baths. The top floor was, at one time, used as a ballroom.

Judge Hallett married the former Katherine Felt in 1882. She died in 1906, and after Judge Hallett's death in 1913, the house was sold by the heirs and was converted to a rooming house, like so many other mansions in Capitol Hill. For years it was operated under the name Wilhite Manor until it was purchased in the early 1970s by Bernie Katz, who restored much of the interior and turned the house into a combination living space and offices.

ADOLPH ZANG HOUSE

Author's Collection

Pillared entrance to the Adolph Zang mansion at Seventh Avenue and Clarkson Street.

Adolph Zang, Denver brewer, banker, and mining man, built this house at 709 Clarkson Street in 1904. He had previously lived at 1532 Emerson Street. Zang was the founder of the Zang Brewing Company, one of the West's largest, located at Seventh Avenue and Water Street, next to the Platte River. Zang originally lived in a house adjacent to the brewery. He was born in 1856 in Kentucky and came West in the early 1870s. After establishing his brewing concern, he widened his interests to include the German American Trust Company and the Schirmer Insurance and Investment Company. Known widely as an astute art collector, he also had an extensive collection of books and manuscripts that he housed in the Clarkson Street mansion.

When Zang died in 1916, his wife, Minnie, continued to live in the house with her small staff until her death in 1950. At that time, the house was purchased by the Western States Mission Church of Jesus Christ of Latter Day Saints. They occupied the mansion for the next three decades until, in the early 1980s, it became home to a number of business offices. It has remained offices since that time.

GEORGE BAILEY HOUSE

Author's Collection

Prominent architect William Lang built this house for George Bailey, one of the best examples of Lang's work still standing.

The imposing three-story, gray, rusticated stone house at 1600 Ogden has been a landmark since it was built in 1889 for local businessman George Bailey. The house is the largest example of architect William Lang's work still in existence. Bailey sold the house after only a few years to Frederick Struby, of the Struby-Estabrook Mercantile Company. The Struby family occupied

Detail of 1600 Ogden Street.

the house until about 1925, and for a time it served as a rooming house.

By the 1930s, the Denver Polyclinic, a group of osteopaths, was operating out of the house. However, many older Denverites will remember it as the Tiffin Inn Restaurant. The Tiffin gained wide popularity under the stewardship of Paul Shank, who also had living quarters on the upper floor of the mansion. For a time, the Denver Art Academy shared space with the restaurant, having moved from its former site at 1026 Seventeenth Street. Business at the Tiffin grew from the late 1940s, when the restaurant opened, until the late 1950s, when it became obvious that a bigger space was needed. The Tiffin vacated the Bailey mansion and moved to the new Writers Manor on South Colorado Boulevard.

Herb Hoard, Denver hypnotherapist and former Tiffin employee, said, "Paul Shank ran a first-class operation. The Tiffin was a place to dress up and go out for an evening of fine dining. He eventually sold out to John R. Thompson of Chicago, who also owned Henrici's. Shank moved from Denver to Scottsdale, where he also did quite well in the restaurant business." The Tiffin closed its doors many years ago.

The Ogden Street property was acquired from the Tiffin in the early 1960s by IntraSearch, Inc., a Denver-based geological consulting firm that used the house as its headquarters for oil and mining exploration. In 1979, the house was sold to ComReal Groups, Inc., a real-estate firm based in Utah with offices in south Denver's Greenwood Plaza. The house became for-lease offices.

Throughout the house's many transitions, much of the interior was mangled. During restoration of the early 1980s, workers removed many coats of paint from the wood paneling throughout the house. It is now offices for Sawaya Rose and Sawaya, Attorneys at Law.

The stairway of the Bailey mansion features a tall, leaded-glass window on its landing.

QUIGG NEWTON/TYSON DINES HOUSE

Author's Collection

712 Corona, the former home of Denver Mayor Quigg Newton.

This house at 712 Corona Street was the home of Denver Mayor Quigg Newton during his term in office, from 1947 to 1955. From a prominent Denver family, Newton graduated from Yale and practiced law before entering local politics. His father, J. Quigg Newton, Sr., was a partner in many of Charles Boettcher's business ventures.

When his term as mayor was up, Quigg Newton became president of the University of Colorado at Boulder from 1956 to 1963. He then returned to law and practiced until his retirement a few years ago. He died in 2003.

This house is now the home of Tyson Dines, descendant of another prominent Denver family.

185

WILLIAM FISHER HOUSE

Author's Collection

The William Fisher house, later the International House, at 1600 Logan Street.

Frank Edbrooke originally designed this 10,563-square-foot residence in 1896 for William Cooke Daniels, son of William B. Daniels, Denver merchandising king and partner of William Garrett Fisher. Daniels chose not to live in the house, and it was sold to Fisher, who moved in with his own family. The Daniels & Fisher concern was, for years, one of the most successful and best-known businesses of its kind. The main store was located at the southeast corner of Sixteenth

is severe, with square angles and large columns facing the west and south. The windows were all of triple-plate glass. The grounds were small and enclosed with a stone and wrought iron wall.

The interior was lavish in its materials and detail. Expensive woods, such as mahogany and walnut, were used for the trim, moulding, and stairwells. Many of the rooms were finished in rosewood or bird's-eye maple. The library on the third floor was paneled in mahogany.

Fisher collected many works of art, among them works by famous artists of the day. After his death in 1897, his widow built a gallery on the north side of the house to display this fabulous collection. The gallery also doubled as a ballroom and was finished in Argentinian satinwood. French mirrors sixteen feet high lined the walls. A stage was built at one end of the room, large enough to hold an orchestra and also to show motion pictures. The house was the center of social activity for years and the scene of some of Denver's most publicized parties.

After Mrs. Fisher, the former Mary Cherry, died in 1937, the house changed hands a number of times. It was, for a time, the headquarters of the Rocky Mountain Motor Tariff Bureau and was later used as offices for the State Education Board. The White Temple, a religious cult, used the mansion for a while before it became the International House in 1958. This was a nonprofit organization that promoted understanding and fellowship among foreigners living in Denver and local citizens.

International House closed in 1975 as a result of declining membership and rising fees. Since that time, the house has been a home base for designers, architects, and a number of other business professionals.

and Lawrence streets. The famous D&F tower, still a landmark on Sixteenth Street, was not built until 1911, after the death of both Fisher and Daniels, Sr.

The house, with three stories and a basement, was built in a modified Greek revival style. It is made of lava stone, quarried near Denver. The exterior design

GEORGE SCHLEIER HOUSE

One of the very last survivors on Grant Street north of Colfax is the George Schleier residence at 1665 Grant, designed in the popular Queen Anne style by prominent architect Frank Edbrooke. Schleier was born in 1827 in Baden, Germany, and settled with his parents in Zanesville, Ohio. As an adult, he left for New York, where he worked for a hat manufacturer before heading west to Kansas. He came to Colorado in the late 1850s and immediately plunged into real estate. He built one of the first two-story structures in the region and later began buying up large parcels of land in the downtown Denver area. He also invested his time and money in freight and mining.

One of his biggest deals was that of the Continental Building downtown. The deal was made on the building and four lots, and when the People's Bank failed to make a success of the venture, Schleier took over with an investment of $4,000. In a few years, it was worth well over half a million dollars.

Schleier was also known as a charitable man, giving his money to many in need around the city and donating generously to the church. He was elected to city council in 1866 and served as city tax collec-

tor. When he died in 1910 at the age of eighty-five, he was one of the wealthiest and most prominent of Denver's citizens. He is buried at Fairmont Cemetery.

His widow, Rachel, continued to occupy the Grant Street mansion after his death. She had a lifelong interest in the city's improvement, and when she died in 1930, her will specified that the bulk of her estate go to the beautification of Denver. Among her bequests was a large sum earmarked for "completion of the civic center, or for the erection in whole or in part of buildings upon or near the civic center, all to become public property owned by Denver." For years, the Schleier Gallery at West Fourteenth Avenue and Bannock Street, adjacent to Civic Center Park, held the core of the Denver Art Museum's collection prior to completion of a new museum building in 1971 on the same site.

The Grant Street mansion was willed to the Catholic Church, and for the next four and a half decades it was the home of the Catholic Charities Diocese of Denver. In the late 1970s, the house was converted to commercial office use and continues in that capacity today.

Author's Collection

The George Schleier residence, 1665 Grant Street.

BIBLIOGRAPHY

BOOKS

William Byers, *Encyclopedia of Biography of Colorado*. Chicago: Century Publishing, 1901.

Gene Fowler, *Timberline. The Story of Bonfils and Tammen*. New York: Covici, Friede, 1933.

Will C. Ferril, *Sketches of Colorado*. Denver: American Printing and Publishing Co., 1911.

John Tebbel, *The Inheritors*. New York: G.P. Putnam's Sons, 1962.

Sally Davis and Betty Baldwin, *Denver Dwellings and Descendants*. Denver: Sage Books, 1963.

Edith Eudora Kohl, *Denver's Historic Mansions*. Denver: Sage Books, 1957.

Who's Who in Denver Society. Press of the W. H. Kistler Stationery Co., 1908.

Who's Who in the Rockies. Denver Press Club, 1923.

Men and Women of Colorado Past & Present. Denver Pioneer Publishing Co., 1944.

James Alexander Semple, *Representative Women of Colorado*. Williamson-Haffner, 1914.

Mrs. Agnes Leonard Hill, *The Colorado Blue Book*. Denver: Ives & Co., 1892.

W.B. Vickers, *History of the City of Denver*. Chicago: Baskin & Co., 1880.

Thomas Noel and Barbara Norgren, *Denver, the City Beautiful.* Historic Denver, Inc., 1987.

Jerome Smiley, *History of Denver.* Times-Sun Publishing Co., 1901.

History of Colorado, Biographical, Vols. 4 and 5. Denver: Linderman Co., 1927.

Phil Goodstein, *The Ghosts of Denver*. Denver: New Social Publications, 1996.

Dick Kreck, Foreword by Thomas Noel, *Murder at the Brown Palace*. Golden, Colo.: Fulcrum Publishing, 2003.

John Litvak, M.D., with David and Jane Litvak, and Ruth Eloise Wiberg, *A History of 1471 Stuart, A Voorhees House*.

NEWSPAPERS

Rocky Mountain News

Denver Post

Denver Republican

Rocky Mountain Herald

Denver Times

Denver Downtowner

Colorado Sun

Denver Daily Times

Cervi's Journal

WEB RESOURCES

www.archives.state.co.us

www.census.gov

OTHER SOURCES

Robinson Maps, 1887

Sanborn Maps, 1901–1929

Baist Maps, 1904

Denver City Directories, 1880–2001

The Denver Building Permits File (before 1908)

Denver Municipal Facts, August 1909, October 1911, January 1912

Colorado Magazine, v. 37, 1959–1960

Echo Magazine (Denver), December 1925

Symposia Magazine (Denver), October/November 1982

M Sharp scrapbook, Denver Public Library Western History Department

Burton scrapbook, Denver Public Library Western History Department

APPENDIX:
NEIGHBORHOOD MAPS

The following maps of Denver's neighborhoods identify the locations of the mansions included in this book. They should provide a useful companion for Sunday drives around the city and a great blueprint for a springtime walking tour.

Those marked with an "E" exist in those locations today. Those marked with a "D" have since been demolished.

NORTH CAPITOL HILL

1 Alexander Craig res. D
   1575 Sherman St.

2 Erastus Hallack res. D
   1701 Sherman St.

3 Charles Thomas res. D
   1609 Sherman St.

4 George Schleier res. E
   1665 Grant St.

5 Peter Gottesleben res. D
   1901 Sherman St.

6 Platt Rogers res. D
   1500 Washington St.

7 Job Cooper res. D
   1500 Grant St.

8 Donald Fletcher res. D
   1575 Grant St.

9 Charles Kountze res. D
   1613 Grant St.

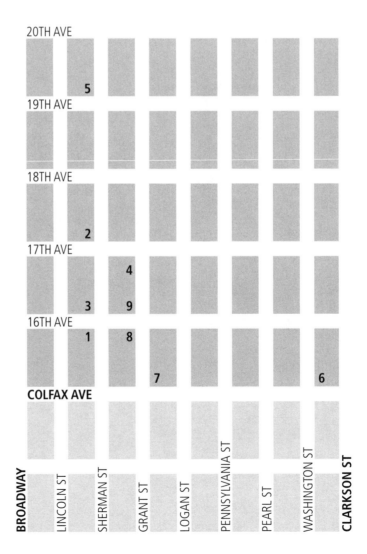

LOWER CAPITOL HILL 1

COLFAX AVE

14TH AVE

13TH AVE

12TH AVE

11TH AVE

10TH AVE

9TH AVE

8TH AVE

BROADWAY · LINCOLN ST · SHERMAN ST · GRANT ST · LOGAN ST · PENNSYLVANIA ST · PEARL ST · WASHINGTON ST · CLARKSON ST

1 John Good res. D
1007 Pennsylvania St.

2 David Moffat res. D
808 Grant St.

3 John Campion res. D
800 Logan St.

4 Charles Boettcher res. D
1201 Grant St.

5 Claude K. Boettcher res. E
400 E. 8th Ave.

6 Charles Boettcher II res. D
777 Washington St.

7 James McClurg res. D
906 Grant St.

8 John Sidney Brown res. D
909 Grant St.

9 Charles Hughes res. D
1200 Grant St.

10 Karl Schuyler res. D
300 E. 8th Ave.

11 Grant/Humphreys res. E
770 Pennsylvania St.

12 J.K. Mullen res. D
896 Pennsylvania St.

13 Horace Bennett res. D
1300 Logan St.

14 William Berger res. D
1170 Sherman St.

15 Molly Brown res. E
1340 Pennsylvania St.

16 Crawford Hill res. E
150 E. 10th Ave.

17 Edwin Hendrie res. E
930 Washington St.

18 Helen Bonfils res. E
707 Washington St.

19 Horace Tabor res. D
1280 Sherman St.

20 Croke/Patterson res. E
428 E. 11th Ave.

21 William Whitehead res. E
1128 Grant St.

22 Dennis Sheedy res. E
1115 Grant St.

23 Walter Dunning res. E
1200 Pennsylvania St.

24 William Friedman res. E
733 E. 8th Ave.

25 Oscar Malo res. E
500 E. 8th Ave.

26 Moses Hallett res. E
900 Logan St.

27 Adolph Zang res. E
709 Clarkson St.

LOWER CAPITOL HILL 2

1 Frederick Bonfils res. D
1500 E. 10th Ave.

2 Frederick Bonfils res. E
1003 Corona St. (1895–1918)

3 Albert E. Humphreys Jr. res. E
1022 Humboldt St.

4 Lawrence Phipps res. D
1156 E. Colfax (1902–1932)

5 William Church res. D
1000 Corona St.

6 Julius Meyers res. D
1205 Ogden St.

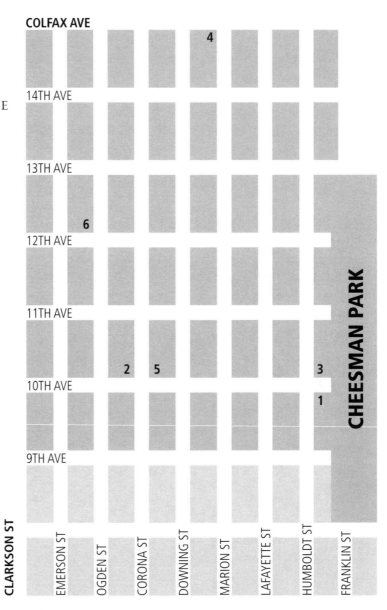

UPPER CAPITOL HILL

with Northeast Capitol Hill & Wyman District

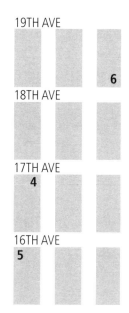

19TH AVE

18TH AVE

17TH AVE

16TH AVE

COLFAX AVE

14TH AVE

13TH AVE

12TH AVE

11TH AVE

10TH AVE

9TH AVE

CHEESMAN PARK

HUMBOLDT ST

FRANKLIN ST

GILPIN ST

WILLIAMS ST

HIGH ST

RACE ST

VINE ST

GAYLORD ST

YORK ST

1 Ed Chase res. D
1490 Race St.

2 Herbert Collbran res. D
1277 Williams St.

3 Owen LeFevre res. E
1311 York St.

4 Isaac Bushong res. E
2036 E. 17th Ave.

5 Castle Marne E
1572 Race St.

6 Eben Smith res. E
1801 York St.

7 Adolph Gustofsen res. D
1470 Gilpin St.

8 Henry Bohm res. E
1820 E. Colfax Ave.

DOWNTOWN DENVER

1 William B. Daniels res. D
1422 Curtis St.

2 George Clayton res. D
1307 Tremont Pl.

3 Amos Steck res. D
1308 Glenarm Pl.

4 Gov. John Evans res. D
1102 14th St.

5 Nathaniel Hill res. D
531 14th St.

6 John S. Brown res. D
1406 Stout St.

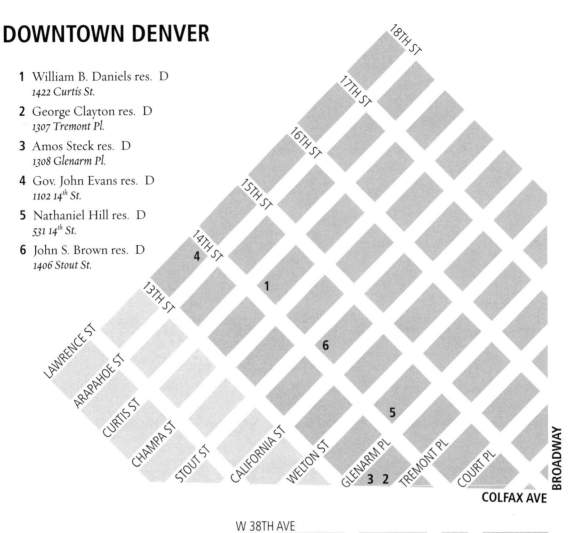

WEST DENVER

1 Ralph Voorhees res. E
1471 Stuart St.

2 John Mouat res. E
2555 W. 37th Ave.

3 Marcus Pomeroy res. D
2949 W. 37th Ave.

4 John B. Walker res. E
3520 Newton St.

INDEX

ignored